O (1-93)

PROFESSIONAL
MAGIC FOR
AMATEURS

PROFESSIONAL MAGIC FOR AMATEURS

Walter B. Gibson

DOVER PUBLICATIONS, INC.
New York

Published in Canada by General Publishing Company, Ltd., 30 Lesmill Road, Don Mills, Toronto, Ontario.
Published in the United Kingdom by Constable and Company, Ltd.

This Dover edition, first published in 1974, is an unabridged and unaltered republication of the work originally published by Prentice-Hall, Inc. in 1947.

International Standard Book Number: 0-486-23012-0
Library of Congress Catalog Card Number: 73-87045

Manufactured in the United States of America
Dover Publications, Inc.
180 Varick Street
New York, N.Y. 10014

PREFACE

DURING thirty-five years of varied experience in magic, the author has witnessed its transition through three distinct stages. In the first of these, the Old School notion still persisted. It furnished three rules on how to become a magician; those rules were: practice, more practice, and still more practice.

Such theory produced many performers who were very skillful at everything except the art of fooling people. So much time was spent in learning intricate sleights and complex routines that a great many students of the art never got around to the fundamental business of doing magic, let alone presenting their wares in entertaining style.

It was only logical that a reaction should occur, as it did. The demand for easier tricks produced a corresponding supply. The incoming epoch provided a new rule; namely, that the best way to learn magic was to begin by doing it. Intriguing in its very nature, this theory took over and with reasonably good results.

For years—perhaps some twenty-odd—the best way to make

a magician was to supply a tyro with a plethora of material which he could develop or discard, as suited his whim. It was a survival of the fittest, in terms of performers rather than their methods, for it could not be expected of a beginner to judge what tricks were best, except in terms of his own limitations.

Tricks themselves demanded only brief explanations, that they might be given a brief test and accepted or rejected according to incomplete returns. Of course the Old School was horrified by the New Era, which in turn scoffed at the Old School. Neither at the time was aware that magic itself was undergoing a period of change.

Good magic will always find its place. This was proven by the fact that newcomers, who favored doing magic rather than practicing its elements, soon began to demand more of themselves. Without a doubt, the greatest proponent of advanced magic was Theo Annemann, a performer who regarded subtlety as the equivalent of skill and proved his point by developing many neglected magical methods into outstanding mysteries.

This demanded a new factor: rehearsal. Today, magic places emphasis upon the psychological factor. The art is actually the matching of wits: those of the performer against his audience. The advantage is all with the magician, provided he makes the most of it. He can do so by planning his work beforehand, testing every important point. This in itself is an acceptance of the old rule that demanded constant practice, but with a very significant difference.

Today, the person who seeks to be a magician is assured of success because the methods he must acquire are within the range of his ability. Skill is often difficult to duplicate, even with the best instruction, whereas subtlety is frequently easy to follow, once its processes are elucidated. The natural magician is invariably versed in both; but natural magicians are comparatively rare.

Hence magic as it stands today affords the perfect opportunity for anyone who seeks to acquire proficiency in the art, since the art itself is based upon subtle method which bears the great part of the burden. Indeed, the term "burden" is a misnomer in itself because it is an interesting adventure to delve into the experiments that constitute the present brand of magic. No such experiment is wasted because it automatically supplies the necessary practice which in a broader sense is actually a form of rehearsal.

The purpose of this book is to introduce the uninitiated into the ways and means of advanced magic with all its practical developments. It therefore will prove of value to persons already acquainted with the art because such a policy has resulted in the inclusion of new effects as well as improvements on certain existing methods.

Since the main purpose is instruction, the author seeks no credit for originality where methods are concerned, though the well-versed reader will unquestionably recognize many instances of such. Rather, all effort has been devoted to blending practicability, ingenuity and novelty into a series of workable effects. The question is not whether tricks should be old or new; but that they should be good.

To make the work comprehensive, simpler tricks are given at the start. These in turn lead into composite effects where ingenuity and novelty are more the trend. Finally, to complete the range of material, the reader is introduced to some of the more spectacular feats of modern magic, great illusions which have been shown on the stage. These will illustrate how the same psychological factors of magic operate on a large scale.

To explain how magic is done is one thing; to tell how to do it, quite another. This volume aims to fulfill the latter and more difficult specification. In keeping with this purpose, each mystery—small or large—is treated as a separate unit, with full descriptions of effect and method, notes on presentation, along with explanatory drawings.

The reader may choose anything from the contents that intrigues him or roam through the book at random, finding workable magic wherever chance or wish may carry him. Each section however is also provided with introductory material covering the particular style of magic found therein, with notes on its general application. These will prove useful in conforming a performance to the circumstances under which it is presented.

CONTENTS

Chapter One

CLOSE-UP MAGIC

Impromptu tricks that will enable you to amaze
your friends while versing yourself in the ways
and wiles of legerdemain.

A simple snap of a handkerchief and a genuine
knot appears instantly!

Inscribed on the back of the hand, then rubbed
away, this mark is found upon the magician's
palm.

Gripped between thumbs and fingers, two
corks are twisted through each other under the
very eyes of all observers.

Turning two strings into one is easy, but only
for those who know how—as others learn when
they try and fail.

Needed for a trick, this match obligingly lifts itself from the box in magical fashion.

Mysteriously, a cigarette rises from a pack at the
magician's command. Done anywhere, any
time, with any pack of cigarettes.

Chapter Two

SIMPLIFIED CARD TRICKS

No skill is required for the card tricks that comprise this section. Self-working, therefore easily learned, they are none the less baffling because of the subtle, unsuspected principles on which they depend.

Chapter Three

CARD-TABLE MAGIC

Specially designed for card table presentation, the tricks in this section are all impromptu effects that can be performed with borrowed packs and exhibited on call.

Chapter Four

AFTER-DINNER MAGIC

A group of tricks with ordinary objects, particularly those found at the dinner table, or which
can be logically introduced there.

Chapter Five

PARTY MAGIC

You can become the life of any party with the tricks described in this section. There are enough of them to give a complete show before a regular audience, yet all the tricks are easy to prepare and simple to perform.

Chapter Six

MENTAL MAGIC

Always intriguing are those tricks that resemble
feats of telepathy or clairvoyance. Here are
methods of performing such mental mysteries
in easy style with baffling results.

Chapter Seven

FAMOUS STAGE ILLUSIONS

CLOSE-UP MAGIC

CLOSE-UP MAGIC

CLOSE-UP or impromptu magic represents one of the real fundamentals in the art of legerdemain. It is necessarily important to the beginner because he must test his aptitude for magic by trying out his first tricks on his friends. Should his small tricks prove successful, he can then proceed safely and with assurance to the performance of larger effects. Conversely, should a few of his impromptu efforts fail him, the budding magician can dismiss them as trivial—even though they were not!—and console himself with the fact that only a few of his intimates caught on to something that he had planned as a real mystery.

Nevertheless, close-up magic should not be considered lightly by the magician himself. It is important for two reasons: first, because it is a real test of magical ability; second, because it is the true mark of the magician. In doing close-up work, the performer is under the sharpest and most critical scrutiny, actually challenging someone to a duel of wits without benefit of dress suit, stage presence, or rabbits. Yet if he had the benefit of all those accoutrements, he could not call himself a magician unless he were able to perform wonders without them!

This is why the person who can learn to perform a few small tricks, and to perform them well, is justly entitled to take his place in the ranks of magic. For he will find himself accomplishing the very results that the greatest professionals in the business are only too willing to seek whenever occasion permits it.

Much of the fame of the Great Herrmann depended upon the fact that he was "always a magician" and therefore ready to perform impromptu miracles whenever he was recognized in public. Thurston and other wizards of a later era gave special attention to certain pet tricks that could be shown on any occasion. Today Blackstone, regarded by many as the greatest magician of all time, is noted for his ability to give a magical performance while surrounded by a dozen people, with the same mystifying results that he obtains upon the stage.

There are magicians who have made of close-up magic an art in itself, notably the famous Jarrow, whose magical conveyance of a fistful of tobacco from one hand to the other has never been duplicated. Here of course we find an instance of unique talent combined with years of arduous practice; but it establishes the fact that certain feats of impromptu magic rate among the greatest mysteries of legerdemain. Nevertheless, a certain basic rule still applies: to be effective, an impromptu trick should be performed with common objects, particularly the sort that could or can be borrowed from the spectators.

This business of employing someone's own weapons, so to speak, disarms him in the same sense. It is the essence of the mystery found in every good feat of close-up magic. Of course the performer can take special advantage of this—as every good magician should—by having a few common articles available in his own pocket. A match box, for instance, is such an ordinary object that why should anyone borrow one to do a trick, provided he already has a match box handy?

That is what the onlooker is supposed to think, and does, which is all the more helpful to the magician when the object he uses is not only his own, but happens to have some special peculiarity suiting it to his own particular purpose. This in itself is something of an insight regarding the wiles of impromptu magic, a feature that will reveal itself more fully as the reader studies the tricks that follow.

Our limitation of this section to tricks with common objects is by no means a restriction. This branch of magic actually affords a greater range and a wider variety of potential deceptions than any other. As a result the tricks described will prove even more selective than might be expected. They have been chosen from among those that require only a modicum of skill, so that the performer can lay all his emphasis upon presentation without worrying too much about the mechanics. Thus he can gain the ease and confidence that come with success in the art of deception, while reserving the time he can devote to practice for some of the more showy effects that will be described in subsequent chapters.

One more observation is needed: since close-up magic is usually shown to a limited group, which may consist even of a single spectator, there is little need to arouse the interest of the spectators or to attract their attention as with a larger gathering. Furthermore, a strictly intimate audience watching close-up magic does not expect too much. Hence incidental tricks or brief surprises, familiarly termed "quickies," often gain surprisingly large proportions in the minds of the observers.

This will account for the inclusion in this section of certain items which at first reading may seem trivial, but which can prove quite baffling in actual performance. Try them and watch the result, always remembering that any indifference displayed by the witnesses may be a reflection of the demonstration itself. If that happens with the trick, the remedy is to try to do it better on the next occasion.

Nor does a single trick constitute a demonstration of magic. One item should follow another, particularly when a certain trick leaves the spectators in a puzzled but probing mood. There is no better way to shake an analytical mind from its purpose than to provide it with something else to worry about. And that epitomizes the whole theme of impromptu magic: don't let your tricks worry you; let them worry your audience!

The Automatic Knot

For a quick, effective, impromptu trick, shaking a knot into the corner of a handkerchief is one of the best.

The Effect

The performer holds a handkerchief so that one corner dangles, lifts that corner and gives it a downward shake. After a few such attempts, a knot suddenly appears in the corner of the handkerchief.

The Method

The knot is secretly tied beforehand, near one of the corners of the handkerchief. That corner is held between the fingers of the right hand so that the knot is hidden in the cupped hand. With his left hand, the performer points to the untied lower corner, then raises that corner to the right hand which takes it between thumb and forefinger. The handkerchief is then given a downward shake, but the knotted end is retained in the cupped fingers of the right hand.

This is repeated two or three times, the left hand always bringing up the loose corner to the right. On the final shake, the right hand retains that corner between thumb and forefinger but opens the other fingers so that the knotted corner flicks downward. By snapping the right hand sharply, the different movements are closely simulated and spectators gain the illusion that the knot actually shakes itself into the corner that originally dangled.

PRESENTATION

Tie a corner of your handkerchief and keep it loosely in your pocket. When you are ready to show the trick, reach into your pocket, find the knot and take it between the fingers of the right hand. Draw the handkerchief from your pocket in a casual manner and you are all ready for the demonstration.

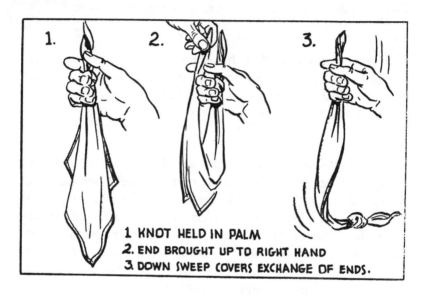

1. KNOT HELD IN PALM
2. END BROUGHT UP TO RIGHT HAND
3. DOWN SWEEP COVERS EXCHANGE OF ENDS.

The Magnetic Mark

Here is a minor miracle employing nothing more than a burnt match and your two hands.

THE EFFECT

With a burnt match, the magician draws a thin line on the palm of his left hand, showing it plainly to his audience. He closes his left hand into a fist and turns it back upward; with the same match he draws a similar line on the back of the left hand, calling attention to the different angle of this line in relation to the hand.

Laying the match aside, the right hand now comes into play. Briskly, its fingers erase the line on the back of the left hand, but with noticeable pressure as though rubbing the mark through the hand itself.

And that is just what happens, magically speaking!

When the left hand is opened, the erased mark has arrived on its palm bisecting the one originally placed there. The fact that both marks are crossed is, according to the magician, obvious proof of the magnetic quality of the inner mark.

THE METHOD

The secret depends upon the placement of the original mark. It is drawn from below the base of the third finger toward the outside of the hand, its midpoint crossing the crease of the palm at an angle.

When the hand is closed tightly, but with fingers straight, not fisted, the mark impresses itself upon the palm, forming a duplicate line at a cross angle to the first. This accounts for the appearance of the second mark.

9

What makes the trick magical is the placing of a mark on the back of the hand and later erasing it. This not only carries the observer's thoughts away from the actual secret; it gives an excuse for closing the left hand.

PRESENTATION

A wooden match is preferable to a paper match. Be sure to allow a good part of the match to burn before extinguishing it so that you will get a nice heavy mark after breaking off the head.

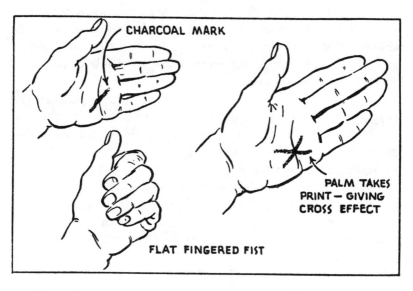

CHARCOAL MARK

PALM TAKES PRINT — GIVING CROSS EFFECT

FLAT FINGERED FIST

This effect, while simple in concept, should be presented in a serious vein to realize its full impact on an audience.

The Twisty Corks

Though other objects can be used for this perplexing trick, corks—and particularly large ones—are best for its demonstration.

THE EFFECT

Two corks are used and one is taken in each hand, gripped in the curve between the base of the thumb and forefinger.

Now, deliberately and without hesitation, the magician brings his hands together, pressing the tips of thumb and second finger of each hand against the ends of the opposite cork, both hands acting simultaneously. The hands are immediately drawn apart with a twist and to the real amazement of the witnesses, the corks are free, each held between its proper thumb and finger, giving the distinct impression that the solid corks were drawn right through each other!

THE METHOD

All depends upon the way the corks are gripped. Hold the left hand palm up and the right hand palm down. Let the right hand approach the left from slightly above so that the right thumb presses the inner end of the left-hand cork. Now it will be found that the left thumb can similarly press the inner end of the right-hand cork.

The right second finger goes to the outside end of the left cork, while the left second finger is swung inward and upward to obtain its grip on the inner end of the right cork. If the hands are then drawn apart with a slight twist, the corks will come along with them.

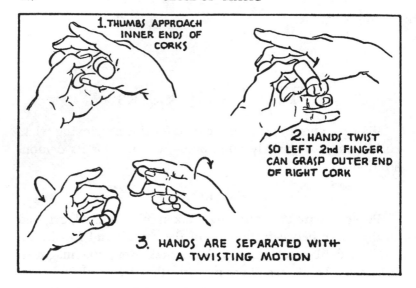

1. THUMBS APPROACH INNER ENDS OF CORKS

2. HANDS TWIST SO LEFT 2nd FINGER CAN GRASP OUTER END OF RIGHT CORK

3. HANDS ARE SEPARATED WITH A TWISTING MOTION

PRESENTATION

This effect should be practiced with reference to the diagrams until the placement of thumbs and fingers becomes automatic. The slight skill required is really preliminary to the part of the trick where observers expect dexterity and this adds to the deception. It is a good repeat trick, but should be demonstrated more rapidly each time.

Spools may be used instead of corks and the trick can be performed nicely with two empty packs of paper matches, each rolled into a loose tube. Once the move is well acquired it can be used with cigarettes or even large wooden matches, but the latter are not recommended as they force the hands into an awkward cramp that spoils the smooth effect.

The Doubled String

Quite different from the usual cut-and-restored effect is this problem of the doubling strings which unite to prove that one and one still make one, but twice as much of it. It is ideal for impromptu work as the effect depends greatly upon having other persons attempt to duplicate the performer's magic but without success; and the participation feature is always desirable in intimate magic.

THE EFFECT

The strings used in this effect are already cut, there being about a dozen pieces, all of about six inches in length, lying handy in a cluster, or the magician may simply bring them from his pocket. These strings are distributed to spectators in pairs, the magician keeping a pair for himself.

Holding his pair between his left thumb and forefinger so that the short ends extend an inch or so above, the magician tells the other persons to do exactly the same. He picks up one long end with the right hand, carries it up to a short end and grips it there with the left fingers; then he similarly adds the other long end to the short end.

Now both hands massage the four string ends between thumbs and fingers, the spectators copying the magician's action with their strings. At the word "pull" everyone is to grip two ends of string and tug them apart. When the magician gives the word, the spectators find that their strings come apart as is to be expected.

But the magician's string stretches itself into one long piece, the pairs having united into a single length which may be examined!

The Method

Special string is required for this mystery, but it is a common type easily obtainable. It should be white cotton of the "stringy" sort, fairly thick; about one-sixteenth of an inch in diameter or heavier and of a loose twist. Experiments with samples of ordinary string will enable anyone to find a suitable type.

Using a twelve-inch length separate the fibers for about two inches at the center, thus forming two equal lengthwise sections. Each of these is doubled and twisted (follow the original twist of the fibers) to resemble two short ends of a string. The performer's string is thus prepared while the pieces to be used by the spectators are merely unprepared six inch lengths.

Placed with the short strings, the specially prepared long one looks enough like the rest to pass casual view. The performer notes the difference however and retains that "pair" while passing out the short ones. He holds his "pair" be-

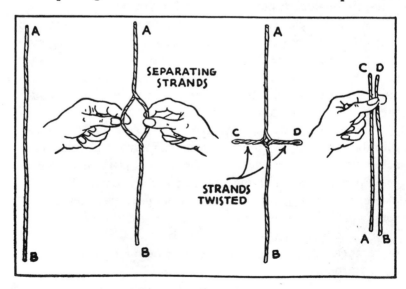

tween the left thumb and forefinger about an inch from the top "ends" which effectively conceals the connection between both pieces.

Thus the performer can apparently display a pair of strings identical to those he has just distributed. He holds these up, shows people how to join the long ends with the short, but in rubbing the four ends together, he retains the long ones. When the performer gives his hands a quick pull apart, the string comes out whole and the doubled loops are drawn taut, thus disposing of the "short ends" that were never there!

PRESENTATION

Here again we have a very mysterious effect which requires little handling on the part of the performer because of previous preparation. At the outset do not make the mistake of calling undue attention to the strings by referring to them as "ordinary" or other similar remarks. In the minds of your audience all strings are ordinary, UNLESS YOU SAY SO!

Pop-up Match

Incidental mysteries are the spice of an impromptu program and the match that pops up when the box is opened comes within this category.

THE EFFECT

Needing a match for a trick or to light a cigarette, the magician takes a box of safety matches from his pocket, pushes the drawer open and, as he does so, a match rises from the rest! The performer removes it and shows it casually, giving the impression that this sort of thing is bound to happen when a magician is around.

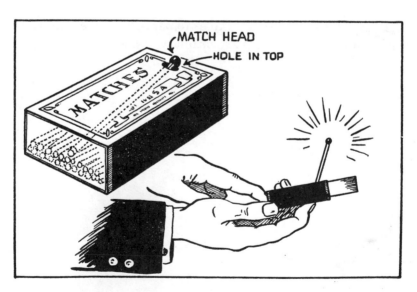

THE METHOD

Simple preparation is required. With a knife point, bore a small hole in the top of a match box cover about a quarter inch from the end. If this hole coincides with some heavily printed portion of the match box label, so much the better. Remove about half the matches from the box, close it, take one of the matches and push it base first into the hole and thus into the drawer until only the head of the match remains in sight where it will not be noticed, being mistaken for part of the label design.

PRESENTATION

In performing, bring out the match box, show it casually, but keep it slightly in motion so that the match head will not be distinguished. Holding the box flat in one hand, push open the drawer from the back with the other hand. Up pops the match, seemingly from among those in the drawer, and the pushing hand promptly draws it free before anyone can note the exact source of its emergence.

If you will tilt the front end of the box slightly upward just as you get ready to push the drawer forward, the illusion of the match actually emerging from the drawer will be heightened.

The Rising Cigarette

An ideal effect in close-up magic is the rising cigarette which slowly emerges from a pack at the performer's command.

THE EFFECT

The cigarette pack is held in the left hand; the right makes mystic passes above it and a cigarette rises straight up to the waiting fingers.

THE METHOD

This trick is literally one that can be done "under a person's nose" because, not only does it need no preparation or special appliances, its method of operation renders it more difficult to detect at very close range.

Here we find an unknown factor helping the deception, always a good point in any trick. The cigarette is not in the pack at all, but is *behind* it, this fact being concealed by using a half empty pack with the empty portion pressed inward at the back to accommodate the odd cigarette.

The front of the pack is against the left fingers, which are pointed straight up toward the top of the pack. The left thumb holds the extra cigarette pressed against the back of the bent-in portion of the empty side of the pack. The lower the thumb, the better, because it provides the motive power by a gradual upward push, the entire action being concealed behind the pack.

This seems so bold at first trial that the effect is not appreciated until you have watched it in a mirror; then the beauty of the illusion will be appreciated.

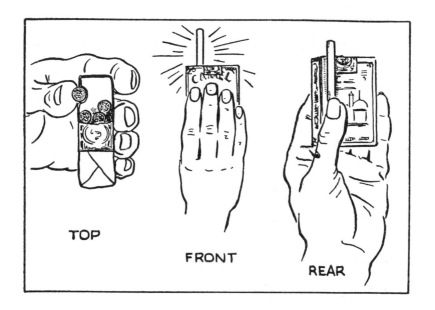

TOP

FRONT

REAR

PRESENTATION

Though simple, the upward movement should be practiced so there will be no awkward cramping of the fingers coincident with the secret motion of the thumb.

There is an added feature with this trick that enables the magician to have it ready for instant use. In opening a cigarette pack, he leaves the cellophane wrapping around it. Then, when the pack is half empty, a cigarette may be inserted downward behind the pack, between the cellophane and the pack proper.

Carried in the pocket, this pack may be brought out at any time with the hidden cigarette already held in place. In this instance, the left thumb does not hold the cigarette at all, but rests below it, so that the thumb-nail can press the cello-

phane below the bottom of the cigarette. Pressing inward
and upward, the thumb forces the cigarette to rise apparently
from the pack, the pressure of the cellophane guiding the
cigarette on its course.

The Chameleon Match

Here is a case where the magician goes against policy and informs his audience exactly what he intends to do before he does it. Of course there are other instances where this is advisable or necessary; but in this trick there is a fell purpose behind the advance information which the magician volunteers. It so happens that he intends to do more than he announces, with the result that an unsuspected surprise awaits the lulled spectators.

THE EFFECT

Taking a match pack from his pocket, the magician removes a match from it, stating that he will demonstrate a peculiarity existing only with red-tipped matches; namely, that by a mere pinch and a pull, the red head can be removed magically from the match.

After a few attempts, the performer grips the match more tightly, gives it a hard tug, and shows that the head is gone. But this flumdubbery leads the spectators to believe that the magician has merely turned the match around, hiding its red tip between his thumb and fingers.

Admitting that the head might be there, the performer does something magical about it. He blows on the match, turns it around and hands it to the spectators. The hidden head is revealed, but it has turned to a *blue* tip instead of a red!

THE METHOD

The result is accomplished by a simple switch of one match (a blue tip) for the original (red tip) first shown to the audience. The blue-tipped match—a loose one—is previously tucked into a partly filled packet of red-tipped matches, which in turn is placed handily in the coat pocket.

In bringing out the packet of matches, the performer acquires the blue-tipped match and holds it between his right thumb and forefinger, the head of the match being gripped while the match proper follows the line of the forefinger, on the inside of the hand, and therefore remains hidden.

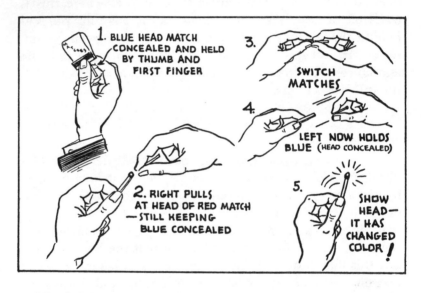

1. BLUE HEAD MATCH CONCEALED AND HELD BY THUMB AND FIRST FINGER

2. RIGHT PULLS AT HEAD OF RED MATCH —STILL KEEPING BLUE CONCEALED

3. SWITCH MATCHES

4. LEFT NOW HOLDS BLUE (HEAD CONCEALED)

5. SHOW HEAD— IT HAS CHANGED COLOR!

The left hand takes a match from the packet (which is held by the right hand). This match, a red tip, is held between the left thumb and forefinger in full view, the thumb and forefinger gripping it by the base. The right hand then tosses the match pack aside.

Now the left hand is showing a red-tipped match projecting from between the thumb and forefinger, while the right hand is concealing a blue-tipped match which points the opposite direction, with its head pressed between the thumb and forefinger, the deeper the better.

Without separating, but merely by compressing further, the right thumb and forefinger go through the pretense of trying to pull the head from the red-tipped match. Not succeeding, the right hand comes further to the left, apparently to gain a full-length draw along the match. The right thumb and forefinger are now above the left, partly covering them. They plant the head of the blue-tipped match between the left thumb and forefinger. Then, transferring their grip to the red-tipped match, the right thumb and forefinger draw it away unseen.

Showing the headless end of the match that is now projecting from his left hand, the magician claims he made the head vanish until hearing doubts from the spectators, he admits that he simply turned it around. He enacts the hocus-pocus already described, or merely opens his fingers and lets the match drop, remarking that in some truly magical fashion, the head has changed color from red to blue, which—now that he remembers it—is what he originally intended to have happen!

PRESENTATION

In making the switch of the matches, do so quite deliberately. It is good to build to this, by doing the whole trick in a fairly deliberate style. Fumbling should be avoided, but is not too serious, because the spectators are supposed to think they have caught on to something.

If need be, the second finger of the right hand can be brought into play, aiding the forefinger in the secret removal of the original red-tipped match, or taking over that task itself, in co-operation with the right thumb.

Immediately after the left hand drops the blue-tipped match on the table, the right hand picks up the match pack and drops it in the pocket, letting the odd red tip fall with it. Another system is to pick up the packet while exhibiting the

"headless" match in the left hand.   Of course it is the right
hand that picks up the packet and calmly pockets it before
the climax of the trick.   In that case it is a good plan for the
right hand to come back and take the match from the left
instead of having the latter drop the match on the table when
the blue tip is shown.

Lacking paper matches of different colors, the trick may
be performed with a *burnt* match.   In such a routine, the
magician explains that he intends to pull away the head—
as usual—and at the finish, he discovers that the head burnt
itself out in some magical fashion while he was bluffing the
spectators with his turn-around stunt.

Ring-a-String

To remove a ring from a string on which it is threaded, while the ends of the string are held by a spectator, is one of those close-up impossibilities that add zest to impromptu magic. Here is the newest and neatest method of accomplishing such a marvel.

THE EFFECT

Taking a candy mint from a package, the perfomer threads it on a thin string. While a spectator holds the ends of the string, the magician covers the candy ring with a handkerchief, reaches beneath the cloth, and a moment later brings out the mint, freed from the string.

The handkerchief is immediately removed, showing the bare string still held by the spectator. Both the string and the mysterious mint may be examined.

THE METHOD

Beforehand prepare a candy mint by breaking it neatly in half. This can be facilitated by placing the mint in a cloth before snapping it. Unless the break is clean, discard this mint and snap another.

Dip the portions of the broken mint in water and then press the ends together. Hold them firmly in place a short while and after that let the mint dry. The mint will not only look quite normal, but will hold together satisfactorily. If cracks show, they can be covered with a tiny application of powdered sugar.

This is the mint which is taken from the package and placed on the string. It can be handled freely and shown fairly closely. In the handkerchief, hidden beneath one folded corner, is a solid mint. Keep this concealed when you drape the cloth over the mint that is on the string.

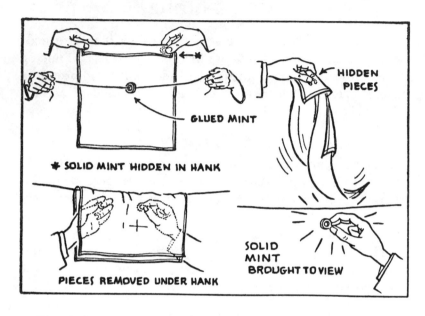

HIDDEN PIECES

GLUED MINT

✱ SOLID MINT HIDDEN IN HANK

PIECES REMOVED UNDER HANK

SOLID MINT BROUGHT TO VIEW

Reach beneath the handkerchief, snap the mint that is on the string. This can be done easily and noiselessly because the break is already there. With one hand bring out the solid mint while the other hand folds another corner of the handkerchief over the broken halves of the original mint and retains them there.

The handkerchief is removed and pocketed, disposing of the broken evidence while the solid mint is given for examination as the original.

PRESENTATION

Several mints may be faked beforehand so as to have them always ready for the trick. However, the trick itself should not be repeated on the same occasion. Follow the method as described but do not state what is to happen until you have covered the faked mint with the handkerchief.

Since you have taken the mint from a regular package and shown it quite freely, everyone will suppose it to be solid. If no mention is made of what is to happen, no one will think of examining the mint until afterward, and then of course a solid mint will be in circulation.

Loop the Loop

There are various stunts with loops of string, some of them involving rings or other objects. Most of these, while puzzling or tricky, tend toward the obvious or are too trivial to produce anything resembling a magical effect. Here, however, is a loop trick which, though brief, is really mystifying with its unexpected result.

The Effect

The performer ties the ends of a piece of string so that it forms an endless loop some twelve inches in length. On this double string he threads a borrowed ring. He asks a person to hold his forefingers or thumbs straight upward. Over them the magician places the ends of the loop, so that it stretches between, the ring hanging in the center.

Now with deft, swift moves, the magician adds more loops over one of the spectator's fingers, by gathering portions of the string and carrying them there. To all appearances this process should tangle the string and perhaps knot the ring on it. Instead, the ring suddenly drops free, leaving the puzzled spectator still staring at the looped string stretched between his extended fingers!

The Method

To practice this trick, fix the loops of the string over the posts of two chairs, unless you have someone to assist you. In either case the loop is hung loosely and all the maneuvers are considered—in terms of left and right—from your viewpoint.

First make sure that the knot on the string is well over to the right. The ring should be hanging from the center of the double string, both strands passing through it.

Reach over with the left hand and with thumb and fore-finger grip the *far* string close to the spectator's finger (which is at the left end of the string). Bring that far string over the near string, then downward and hold it taut.

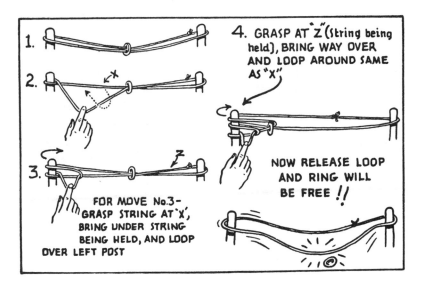

Your right hand then takes the other string (originally the near strand) a trifle further to the right. With right thumb and forefinger, this string is brought *over* the string your left hand is holding. It is looped around the spectator's finger at your left.

Now the right hand moves over to the right, traveling beyond the ring. Plucking the far string, your right hand carries it clear to the left and loops it over the spectator's finger, just as with the loop that was previously placed there.

Your left hand next releases the string that it is holding. The ring, which has been drawn somewhat to the left, will begin sliding toward the center of the string. Your right hand should go below to catch it, because the ring will now drop clear, leaving the string still stretched between the surprised spectator's fingers!

No loops have been removed; instead, two have been added, which makes the trick all the more effective. Practice the moves until they can be done smoothly, and the presentation will take care of itself!

SIMPLIFIED CARD
TRICKS

SIMPLIFIED CARD TRICKS

NO BRANCH of magic has a wider range than that of wizardry with cards. In fact, card magic can justly be said to form a field all its own and it is more than likely that the tricks in this one category outnumber the combined total of items in all other branches.

It is the very wealth of material found in card magic that renders it attractive to the newcomer. However, to begin such a study on his own would entangle him in a maze of fancy shuffles, difficult flourishes and complicated sleights from which he might never extricate himself.

In the old days it was customary to teach card magic the hard way. The result was that students became strong on manipulations but weak on magic where cards were concerned. Simple card tricks requiring no skill were either looked upon in contempt or almost totally overlooked.

The word "almost" is important, because it represents the saving factor that brought about a whole new art in card conjuring. Certain performers, introducing simpler tricks haphazard fashion, or simply as novelties amid their more serious efforts, discovered that some of these neglected items carried more mystery and audience appeal than did the skillful sleights. That set inventive minds to work along a new direction, with the result that subtlety soon replaced skill in the creation of new card marvels.

Today, a person has only to be familiar with a pack of cards to begin doing magic with it. He should be able to shuffle a pack neatly and deal cards rapidly, as a proficient card player would. In brief, spectators do not expect a magician to be clumsy with the objects that he handles.

There are two varieties of shuffles: the dovetail and the overhand. In the dovetail, each hand takes half the pack and the thumbs riffle the inner ends of the packets so that the cards interlace when falling. In the overhand, the ends of the pack are held between thumb and fingers of one hand, which is beneath the pack; while the thumb of the other hand peels off cards in little clusters letting them drop into the bend of the fingers until the whole pack has arrived there. The first hand assists this by drawing away each time the other hand peels off a cluster.

Versed in such ordinary methods of handling a pack, the reader will require very little additional skill to perform the simplified card tricks described in this section. The tricks themselves have been selected because of their deceptive qualities and any complicated phases have been replaced by simple yet effective devices. In some instances, further suggestions involving some special artifice are added to the comments on presentation, so the reader can try a more advanced version if he desires; but these addenda depend on timing or misdirection rather than skill.

All the card tricks in this section are the sort that can be done almost anywhere under about any reasonable conditions.

Therefore dealing tricks, or those in which layouts are required, have been reserved for a later section of tricks suitable for the card table.

In the present group, where reference is made to laying cards on a table, not only any handy table may be used, but the cards may be placed on a chair, on a spread-out paper, or in some cases on the floor or in a spectator's hands. Such informal presentation is often helpful to a magical effect, causing spectators to assume that great skill must be required because the conditions themselves appear difficult.

The smart magician should never shatter such opinions, but instead should take advantage of all mistaken notions to put across his simplified card tricks under the guise of demonstrations requiring the utmost in technique.

Faces Up!

Based upon a very deceptive principle, this startling effect has been reduced to a simplicity of detail which renders it positive of operation at first trial. Study the effect, test the method exactly as described, and the trick will be ready for performance.

THE EFFECT

After shuffling a pack of cards a spectator gives one half to the magician and retains the other half for himself. The magician and the spectator turn their backs so that each can remove and remember a card from his own half. When they face each other again, they are each holding a packet of cards face down in one hand, with an odd card face down in the other hand.

Giving his card to the spectator, the magician tells him to push it face down in his packet. That is, the spectator's packet receives the magician's card, pushed therein by the spectator himself. Similarly, the magician takes the spectator's card and pushes it into his—the magician's—packet, face down.

Thus two chosen cards—one known to the spectator, the other to the magician—have been buried in separate packets, making it quite difficult to find them. However, to convince people further, the magician holds his own packet face down in one hand, takes the spectator's packet in the other and, behind his back, places the two packets together. Then, turning so that observers can see the assembled pack, the magician cuts it a few times behind his back.

Placing the pack face down on the table, the magician

announces the name of the card he looked at—say, the eight of spades. He asks the spectator to name his card, which we will suppose to be the three of clubs. Tapping the pack two times—once for each card—the magician gives the whole pack a wide spread, or lets someone run through the cards.

Two cards are found face up in the pack. They are the chosen eight of spades and the three of clubs!

THE METHOD

The deception actually begins before anyone suspects it, namely, when the magician turns away to remove and remember a card from his packet. Free from observation, the magician turns his entire packet *face up*, then takes one card —in this case the eight of spades—and places it *face down* upon the inverted packet.

This is the card that the magician remembers. However, he takes *another* card and turns it face down in his other hand. Thus when he again confronts the spectator, the magician is holding a face-up packet disguised by the face-down eight of spades on top, while in his other hand he has an indifferent face-down card. It is this odd card that the magician gives the spectator so the latter can place it in his packet.

Meanwhile, the magician is taking the spectator's face-down card (the three of clubs) and is pushing it into his own packet, which he keeps well squared so that no one will notice that only its top card, and the one handed over by the spectator, are actually face down.

At this point the proper way for the performer to hold his packet is with his hand **palm up**, the packet resting above between the thumb at one side and the fingers at the other. Taking the spectator's packet in similar fashion, the magician places both behind his back. In so doing, he *turns over* his own packet in putting it on the spectator's. Now the whole pack is properly assembled, but in it are two face-up cards: the eight of spades which topped the performer's packet and the three of clubs, which the spectator looked at and which was buried in the performer's batch of cards.

His back turned to the spectators, the magician lets them watch him cut the pack. He should do this twice; the first time cutting deep into the pack, lifting about two-thirds of it;

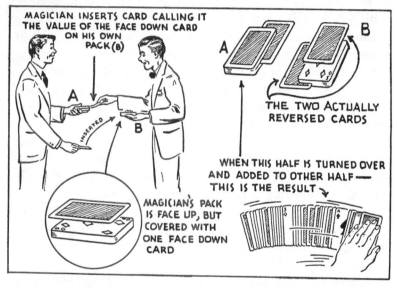

MAGICIAN INSERTS CARD CALLING IT THE VALUE OF THE FACE DOWN CARD ON HIS OWN PACK (B)

A

B

INSERTED

B

A

B

THE TWO ACTUALLY REVERSED CARDS

WHEN THIS HALF IS TURNED OVER AND ADDED TO OTHER HALF—THIS IS THE RESULT

MAGICIAN'S PACK IS FACE UP, BUT COVERED WITH ONE FACE DOWN CARD

the second time, cutting only about a dozen cards from the top. Now when the pack is placed on the table or handed to a spectator, it is all set for the "magic taps" that will cause the buried cards to show themselves. But first those cards must be named. So the performer boldly says: "The card I gave you was the eight of spades. What card did you give me?"

The spectator names the three of clubs and the trick is as good as done, nobody realizing that the magician *miscalled* his card, naming one that he had fixed on his own packet instead of the unknown card he gave the spectator. When the spectator's card shows face up in the pack, everyone takes it for granted that the magician's card did a similar flip-over, since the card he named shows face up too.

PRESENTATION

Well covered in the description of the method, the presentation calls for only one reminder.   In placing the two sections of the pack together, the performer should be facing the audience as he puts the halves behind his back, thus hiding the turnover of his own packet.   However, he should immediately swing around so that people can see the assembled pack before he would have time for any intricate manipulations.

A variant or bolder method is to assemble the packets without placing them behind the back.   In this case, as the performer reaches for the spectator's packet with one hand, he brings his own packet forward with a sweep, turning over his hand—and the packet—as he does so.   Properly timed, this maneuver will never be detected, but the performer should be sure of its execution before attempting it.

In performing this effect be sure to use a pack which has a white margin all around it, otherwise the presence of an inverted card may be detected.   White-margin cards are very common and therefore usually available.   The trick can be worked with other packs but great care must be taken to keep the cards perfectly squared during all the vital stages.

The Wandering Colors

For a direct effect with a startling climax, this peculiar transposition of two groups of cards—reds and blacks—would be difficult to equal. Yet in actual performance it is practically self-working, requiring only a brief rehearsal toward presenting it convincingly.

THE EFFECT

Sorting through a pack of cards, the performer forms the reds and blacks into different groups. Then, turning the cards with their faces toward the spectators, he runs slowly through the pack, thumbing the cards one by one so all can see the result. The lower half of the pack consists entirely of reds; the upper half of blacks. Turning the pack toward him, the performer separates the two halves and shuffles each individually, placing the groups side by side on the table, face down.

Picking up one heap, the magician looks through it until he finds a king which he lays face up with the packet face down beside it. Thus the king of spades, placed beside such a packet, would represent the black half of the pack. From the other heap he takes a king and does the same, thus representing the red heap by such a card as the king of hearts.

Now the performer states that to transfer all the cards from one heap to the other, one card at a time, would require twenty-five exchanges. He illustrates this by turning up a black card and a red, then putting them in the opposite heaps, face down. But there is an easier way to accomplish it, namely, by magic.

To prove this, the magician takes the black king and pokes

it face up in the red heap. He then pushes the red king face up in the black heap. Turning the two heaps over, the magician spreads them and to everyone's amazement, the heap containing the king of spades has turned entirely black, while the king of hearts has drawn all the red cards to its group!

THE METHOD

In sorting the reds and the blacks, the magician does a bit of preliminary fixing, which is not noticed because he keeps the faces of the cards toward himself. He arranges the reds at the bottom of the pack, that is, the first cards fronting toward him, with the blacks constituting the upper or rear section.

However, the performer is careful to slip two red cards clear to the top or back of the pack. One of these must be a red king—such as the king of hearts—the other simply any red spot card.

Also, in arranging the black half, the performer sees to it that the two front cards—those that will be at the very middle of the entire pack—consist of a king—such as the king of spades—and a black spot card.

When he runs through the pack to show how he has segregated the reds and blacks, the performer is quite safe until he nears the finish, where two red cards are hidden behind the blacks, at the top. However, the performer does not need to run that far because by the time he nears the top he has shown quite clearly that the reds and blacks are separated.

To prevent any slip, it is a good plan to extend the left forefinger beneath the pack at the back and crook it up around the last few cards. Thus that portion of the pack is held in a sort of clamp and there will be no danger of exposing the pair of hidden red cards.

The next maneuver is to spread the pack quite widely at the center, almost dividing the reds from the blacks. The visible reds, the near portion of the pack, are resting mostly on the right hand; the blacks on the left.   But beneath this face-up spread, the fingers of the right hand should actually press up beneath the two front cards of the black group, so they can be drawn away with the red packet.

This is done when the performer tilts the pack toward himself, showing the backs instead of the faces.   All in the same motion he draws the halves apart, saying he will divide the reds from the blacks.   Thus, when he turns the heaps face down and lays them apart, one group consists of red cards topped by a black king and spot; the other is composed of black cards, topped by a red king and spot.

Just in case someone might remember which heap is which, the performer shuffles one face down, replaces it on the table, picks up the other and shuffles it.   He repeats this while explaining that he is about to test a peculiar scientific principle that applies to colors.

Finishing with one heap in his hands, the performer notes

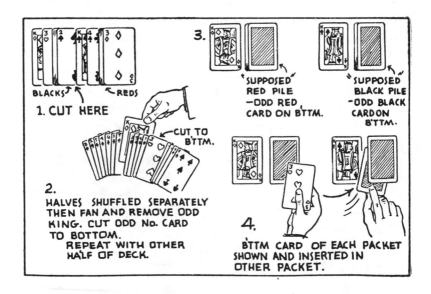

BLACKS   REDS

1. CUT HERE

CUT TO BTTM.

2.
HALVES SHUFFLED SEPARATELY THEN FAN AND REMOVE ODD KING. CUT ODD No. CARD TO BOTTOM.
    REPEAT WITH OTHER HALF OF DECK.

3.

"SUPPOSED" RED PILE —ODD RED CARD ON BTTM.

"SUPPOSED" BLACK PILE —ODD BLACK CARD ON B'TTM.

4.
BTTM CARD OF EACH PACKET SHOWN AND INSERTED IN OTHER PACKET.

its general color, then names the *opposite,* stating: "From this black heap I shall take a king and place it face up, to indicate the color of the heap." He finds the king of spades (which was plucked away with the red cards) and lays it face up on the table. Then he cuts the packet at the *other* black card, bringing it to the bottom, so that in squaring the packet he can casually show what appears to be a black heap, before laying it face down beside the king of spades.

Picking up the other half of the pack, the performer repeats his statement, this time referring to a red heap. From it he places the king of hearts face up, cuts at the one red-spot card, bringing it to the bottom. Thus he can show the "red" heap as he terms it.

Now comes the business of the transfer. Lifting the "black" heap slightly, the performer uses his other hand to draw the bottom card from beneath. He lays down the heap, shows the face of the black card he has drawn and pushes that card in the "red" heap. Immediately he draws the bottom card from the "red" heap, shows its face and puts this red card into the "black" heap.

Tested with the cards in hand, this whole process becomes self-explanatory. By transposing the two decoy cards, the magician has not only convinced the onlookers that the red heap is with the red king and the black heap with the black king; he has disposed of the only two cards that prevented the situation from being just the opposite.

All is therefore ready for the startling climax. Rather than waste time in transposing cards one by one, the performer resorts to magic. He states that the mere transposition of those face-up kings will attract all the remaining cards of their particular colors. To prove this, he pushes the king of spades face upward in the "red" heap and the king of hearts is similarly inserted in the "black" heap.

The trick is then done. It remains only to add a few

dramatic gestures, such as sliding the packets further apart, wigwagging the hands from one to the other, and finally giving each group a separate spread to show the remarkable result.

The Names Tell

As a mental coincidence this trick stands unrivaled because there are three chance factors concerned. Of course actually nothing is left to chance, because there is a trick to it. The basic principle, however, is subtly concealed; but even more remarkable, the whole trick appears to be done by the spectators themselves. This means in turn that no skill is required, but the mystery is too good to be spoiled by any hesitancy or carelessness; therefore its presentation should be well rehearsed.

THE EFFECT

A person is asked to shuffle a pack of cards; then to count off a small number of cards—under a dozen—and place them in his pocket. This is done while the performer's back is turned and to make sure that he will remember his number, the spectator is asked to count off the same quantity of cards again.

This new group is not to be pocketed. Instead, the performer—his back still turned—carefully explains that the spectator is to square these cards in a little packet, note the card on the face, or bottom, of that packet and then replace the packet itself on the deck. He can let other people see the card that he noted, but after replacing the packet, the whole deck should be squared so that the performer can not guess how many cards were removed.

Taking the pack, the performer holds it face down and asks three other people to call out names at random. These are to be first or given names and nicknames are banned. For instance "James" would be used instead of "Jim." We will suppose that the names announced are James, Louise and Richard.

The performer states that he wants each person to take the pack in turn and spell the particular name that he selected, dealing a card for each letter. To illustrate this, the performer spells the names himself, one after the other, precisely as the spectators are to do. He hands the pack to the person who looked at a card and tells him to bring those odd cards from his pocket and replace them on the pack so it will be complete. That done, the pack is passed around the circle and the persons who picked the names spell them: first J-A-M-E-S; then L-O-U-I-S-E; finally R-I-C-H-A-R-D.

With a pencil, the performer pushes the next card from the top of the pack without even touching any of the cards themselves. He asks the original spectator to name the card he looked at, which we will presume was the jack of diamonds. The person is told to turn up the card that was pushed from the pack.

Turned up, the card proves to be the jack of diamonds!

The Method

This trick is very nearly automatic, but close attention must be given to certain details, particularly one in which the performer himself figures. First, the spectator removed and pocketed a small number of cards; then counted the same number and noted the bottom card of that group before replacing it on the pack. At this point, the original batch must still remain in the spectator's pocket.

The names are given after the performer takes the pack. In explaining how they are to be spelled the magician does so himself, quite openly, since he is merely showing how. In this spelling, the performer draws off one card after another, letting each succeeding card fall on the one he drew

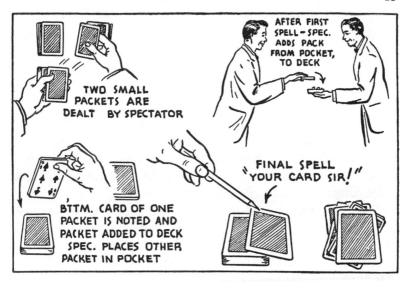

TWO SMALL
PACKETS ARE
DEALT BY SPECTATOR

AFTER FIRST
SPELL – SPEC.
ADDS PACK
FROM POCKET,
TO DECK

BTTM. CARD OF ONE
PACKET IS NOTED AND
PACKET ADDED TO DECK
SPEC. PLACES OTHER
PACKET IN POCKET

FINAL SPELL
"YOUR CARD SIR!"

ahead of it. That is, he reverses the order of those cards, from top to bottom, as he deals them.

This is essential to the success of the trick so it must be done naturally. The best way is to draw a card with the right thumb and let it fall into the bend of the fingers, so that the next card will simply drop upon it. Or the cards can be dealt one by one on the table, each card going on the one ahead. The whole group is then replaced upon the pack and the performer states that the persons are to spell the names themselves.

Here however the magician gives the pack to the party who looked at the chosen card and tells him to put back those odd cards that are in his pocket, replacing them on top of the pack. Done at this point, that action completes the set-up and from then on the result is sure, provided the performer watches against any spectators bungling their spelling.

PRESENTATION

Most of the presentation is covered in the method, but there are other points that insure or help the mystery. First, the trick depends upon the fact that the total number of letters in the names is greater than the number which the first man counted.

The specification to count off "less than a dozen" usually fixes matters so that the names will letter up to a larger total: for example, James, Louise, Richard total eighteen letters. However, in case this total threatens to be short, simply ask a fourth person to supply a name.

In explaining about the spelling—and thereby maneuvering the reverse count—the performer should address the spectators: "I want you to spell the names *yourselves*—exactly like this—J-A-M-E-S—a letter for each name——" and so on. Afterward people will forget that the performer spelled the names at all and those who do remember will not realize that he accomplished anything thereby, since the spectators themselves spelled those names later.

For the final effect, it is wise to sum the entire situation before turning up the card that was pushed aside. The performer can state: "Remember, I have no idea what number was originally counted. I have not seen the chosen card. The names were suggested entirely by other people, who spelled those names themselves. Only by sheer coincidence could all those things correspond. And yet——"

With that, the performer asks the name of the chosen card. When the first man says "jack of diamonds" the performer gestures to the lone card and says "Turn it up." When the card proves to be the diamond jack, the magician can blandly add: "I call it mental coincidence."

Note: Mathematically, the trick can be analyzed thus: consider the total letters in the names as a group in itself. Suppose that the first man originally counted eight cards down.

The chosen card is therefore the eighth card from the top in the name group. Reversing the deal by the preliminary spelling puts the card eight from the bottom in the name group. But the first man has that identical number of cards —eight—in his pocket and when he replaces these on the pack before the spectators start to spell, he makes up for the eight cards at the bottom of the name group and the spelling ends just before the selected card.

Predicted Colors

Suitable for performance at the card table as well as with a regular routine, this trick also comes within the range of Mental Magic, hence is appropriate in connection with such effects. While not as startling as some card effects, it strikes a perplexing note and its ease of operation gives it a sure result.

THE EFFECT

After a spectator has shuffled a pack, the magician takes a quick glance through the cards, then lets the spectator have one more shuffle. Meanwhile, the performer writes a prediction on a slip of paper which he lays close at hand.

Next, the performer tells the other person to start dealing cards in pairs. Every time he comes to two blacks, he is to lay them in one pile; every pair of reds goes in another. Should a pair come red and black, it is placed in a discard heap.

The person proceeds thus through the entire pack. After he has finished, he is invited to open the slip of paper. On it he finds written: "You will have two more reds than blacks." Counting the red group and the black group, the spectator finds that the prediction is correct!

THE METHOD

Two elements are combined in this trick to turn a simple problem into a real perplexity. Its basis is that if the red and black cards were simply separated from a pack, the heaps would come out even. To disguise this well-known fact, the performer has the spectator form his heaps in pairs of reds and blacks, eliminating any that do not conform. This gives the process an irregularity that makes an uneven result seem logical.

Nevertheless, the pairs of reds and blacks should come out equally, for the discards are pairing off too, and therefore have a bearing on the totals only. The performer knows this, but the spectator is thrown off the trail, particularly when the

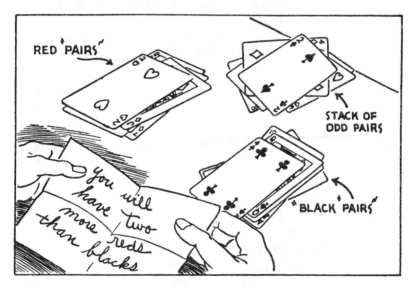

RED "PAIRS"

STACK OF ODD PAIRS

"BLACK" PAIRS

You will have will more two than reds blacks

red and black heaps come up with different totals in keeping with the prediction.

That brings us to the second element: the prediction. It is a subtle feature in itself. Inasmuch as the spectator is pairing cards, not counting them, he never checks the total of the pack and the discards, ignored later, prevent him from so doing when he counts the segregated reds and blacks.

To set the prediction for "two more reds," the performer merely removes two black cards from the pack before beginning the trick. This is done secretly, of course, either well beforehand, or during some opportunity after another trick. Whatever the total of the black heap, it will lack that pair. Thus the result will be two more reds than blacks.

Later the performer should add the missing cards. If he wishes to repeat the trick after an interval, he should make a different removal. Two reds removed will mean "two more blacks than reds." Or the performer may take four or even six of one color, in which case he varies his prediction accordingly, in favor of the other color.

PRESENTATION

The whole effect should be presented as though it were quite difficult in order to cover the simple factors actually involved. The performer can run through the pack beforehand, as if committing cards to memory; then keep close watch while the spectator shuffles.

Glancing through the pack, then allowing a final shuffle, is also a bit of business that helps the effect. Also, the performer can hold his prediction until after the spectator has done the pairing process with about a dozen cards. Such embellishments of course depend upon the individual performer as well as his audience.

Turning away as if to arrange the pack beforehand and thus prepare for some intricate calculation is also a good way of pocketing some cards unnoticed. After the trick, the entire pack can be pocketed; then, when brought out for another trick, the missing cards can be brought along with it.

Slip-Slap

This is a wonderful trick because the worse you do it the better it is. That also makes it a nice trick for beginners, but advanced performers will find it worthy of presentation because of the surprise result. Of course the phrase "the worse you do it" still means that you must do it right; but you'll find that very easy. The trick looks haphazard and careless, which is how it gets its title.

THE EFFECT

A shuffled pack is cut into two heaps. A person looks at the card on one heap; then, leaving that heap face down, he places the other heap face up, on top of it. The magician picks up the pack and proceeds to peel off cards in little clusters, turning some face up, some face down, until the pack is a conglomerate mass of face-up and face-down cards.

To conclude this, the haphazard wizard cuts the pack and slaps one batch on top of the other, which should mess the arrangement all the more. But when he gives the pack another slap with his hand, a strange result takes place.

Spread out, the cards have somehow managed to adjust themselves. No longer are they sandwiched face up and face down. All are one way, face down, exactly as a well-behaved pack should be, but with a solitary exception.

In that pack a single card reveals itself face up and by some happy coincidence it proves to be the very card that the spectator chose!

THE METHOD

It's all in the handling of the cards and since they are handled in such slap-happy fashion it is obvious that no great skill is required. But the performer must be careful to mix the pack exactly as to be described.

Hold the pack in the left hand, thumb across the top, fingers beneath the bottom. The top half of the pack will be face up, as replaced by the spectator. The right hand approaches from its side of the pack, thumb above, exactly like the left hand. The right hand peels off a few cards; then the hand turns over, cards and all, and slaps those few cards face down on the pack.

Meanwhile, the left thumb is pushing a few more cards to the right. The right hand takes those along with the original batch, as it draws away, thumb down. The right hand turns thumb upward, slaps its cards on the pack and gathers away a few more which are helped by a shove of the left thumb.

The right hand continues this constant turn-over process, giving the impression that batches of cards are being drawn away alternately face up and face down. So they are, but they are forming into two distinct groups, a solid sector of face-down cards upon a similar stack of face-up cards. In brief, the pack is not being jumbled as the observers suppose.

As the slip-slap process nears the center of the pack, finishing with the half that was originally face up, the right thumb must be upward for the final draw. This is important, because as the right hand draws off the last of the face-uppers from the pack, it takes along the first face-down card from the lower half. This happens to be the chosen card, but that fact is not mentioned. Quite to the contrary, it is good practice to slide that card unnoticed beneath the others. This is not difficult, with the left thumb aiding and the more carelessly it is done, the better it is covered.

Holding his hands just as they are, both with thumbs upward, the magician notices that the cards in his left are face down, so to complicate matters further, he turns over that group in the left hand, kicking the packet from beneath with his left thumb.   The heap in the left hand is now face up and the left thumb promptly pushes a few of these cards *beneath* the batch in the right hand, where they are gathered by the right fingers.

From then on, the right hand resumes its sloppy shuffle, turning thumb down, thumb up, and so on, drawing away

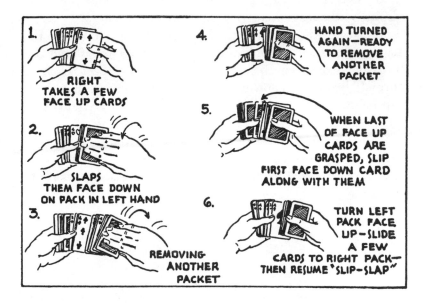

1. RIGHT TAKES A FEW FACE UP CARDS

2. SLAPS THEM FACE DOWN ON PACK IN LEFT HAND

3. REMOVING ANOTHER PACKET

4. HAND TURNED AGAIN—READY TO REMOVE ANOTHER PACKET

5. WHEN LAST OF FACE UP CARDS ARE GRASPED, SLIP FIRST FACE DOWN CARD ALONG WITH THEM

6. TURN LEFT PACK FACE UP—SLIDE A FEW CARDS TO RIGHT PACK— THEN RESUME "SLIP-SLAP"

little batches from the cards in the left hand.   But the procedure as described has masked the chosen card completely. Furthermore, when the so-called shuffle is completed, the pack, instead of being badly jumbled, will consist of two halves: the top face down, the bottom face up.

Announcing that he has jumbled the cards beyond ordinary reclaim, the performer states that he will complete the ruin by cutting the pack and adding to the general mix-up.   He holds his hands close together, thumbs up, and spreads the

pack very slightly at the center, so as not to expose other portions of the two halves.

Finding the break, where face-down cards encounter face-
up, the magician cuts the pack at that point, turns over the
top half and slaps it bodily upon the lower half.   With his
left hand he turns over the entire deck, thumb-kick fashion,
and the right hand gives the pack another slap.   This blow
from the right palm is the magic stroke that produces strange
results, so the magician says—and proves.

Spreading the pack slowly from top toward bottom, the
magician calls attention to the fact that all the face-down
cards have reversed themselves, bringing the pack back to
normal; but as he continues, the performer adds that there
will be one exception, the chosen card, which invariably prefers to remain face up and thus declare its identity.

Sure enough, the chosen card alone is found face up, provided the performer has followed the routine throughout,
and its discovery climaxes an already baffling demonstration.

The Magic Deal

Read this trick carefully, then try it—on yourself. You will find that it is a rare gem, magically speaking; a self-baffling trick. Of course when you perform it publicly you should take credit for accomplishing something wonderful. Then you will fool your audience doubly.

THE EFFECT

Dealing three heaps of seven cards, face down, the magician asks someone to pick up a heap, look at its cards and remember any card he wishes. He is then to place the heap face down between the other two, sandwich fashion.

Again the cards are dealt in three heaps, in rotation; that is, a card for the first heap, one for the second, one for the third; then one for the first, second, third, and so on. The cards are always dealt face down, succeeding cards being placed upon those already dealt.

Now the spectator guesses which heap his card is in and looks to see if he is right. Having found the heap which contains his card, it is placed between the other two. Again the stack is dealt in three heaps exactly as before and the spectator makes another guess as to which heap contains his card.

Finding that heap, the performer takes it face down. In fact, all through the trick the performer has kept the faces of the cards away from him, unless testing the trick with himself as spectator. Now the performer begins to spell some words and with each letter, he transfers a card from the top of the heap to the bottom. At the end of each word he deals a card face down on the table and continues the spelling process with the cards that remain.

Here are the words the magician spells. Each capital letter represents the transfer of a card from top to bottom of the heap. Each star represents a card dealt on the table:

T-H-I-S-*-I-S-*-T-H-E-*-C-A-R-D-*-Y-O-U-*-T-O-O-K-*

When he reaches the word "took" the performer will be working with only two cards, transferring each from top to bottom in turn. So when he deals a card after spelling "took" he will have only one card left.

Naturally, the magician can't do any more spelling with just one card. So he turns up the card.

It will be the card the spectator took!

THE METHOD

That's it. Just do the trick as described and it will wind up with the chosen card. Three deals: after the first and second, the heap with the chosen card goes between the other

two; after the third deal, spell and discard with the heap that holds the chosen card. The result is always the same.

A few details should be noted, however, all necessary to the method and therefore incorporating presentation. The cards can be handled rather carelessly until they are gathered for the second deal. Then the heap with the chosen card must go between the other two and after the second deal, the order of cards must not be disturbed.

Therefore it is not wise to let the spectator handle the cards after they have been dealt the second time. Instead, ask him to guess which heap his card is in; then pick up that heap and spread its cards fan fashion with the faces toward him, so the spectator can see if his card is there or not.

If the card is there, close the fan and place the heap between the other two. If it is not there, lay down the heap, let him choose another, and spread it before the spectator's eyes. If he sees the card, close the heap and put it between the other two. If it is not there, simply pick up the third heap—which must contain his card—and without bothering to spread it, plant it face down between the other heaps.

After the third deal, fan the heaps one by one before the spectator until he sees his card. Then turn the heap face down and go into the final spelling stunt. If the card isn't in the first two heaps you show him, simply spell with the third, face down, without showing its cards to the spectator.

Your excuse for all this is to find out how good a guesser he is. If he picks the right heap after the second deal, you say you will deal the cards and let him try it again, to see if his luck can hold. If he doesn't pick the right heap on his first guess after the second deal, tell him you will deal the cards again and give him another chance.

CARD-TABLE MAGIC

CARD-TABLE MAGIC

I T IS a curious fact that the average magician, when called upon to perform tricks at a card table, is apt to call upon almost every type of appliance except that most readily at hand—a pack of cards.

This might indicate that magicians are so rarely asked to participate in card games that they find themselves in an unfamiliar environment, but such an answer is too facetious to fit the case. However unfamiliar certain magicians may be with certain card games, most of them know a multitude of card tricks. So we are back to the original question: Why not do card tricks?

The reason many magicians don't, is because very few of the usual card tricks are suited for performance at a table. Often a magician finds it convenient to move from one person to another; on other occasions, he accomplishes some secret maneuver while turning away; or there are times when he must hold a pack of cards so that only he can see the faces. These operations prove rather difficult at the card table, particularly if interested parties are kibitzing over the magician's shoulder.

So magicians are prone to adapt dinner-table tricks to card-table presentation, which is also apt to prove unfortunate, since suitable objects are lacking and the conditions are too variable. So perhaps we have found the real reason why some magicians avoid card games. They may be apprehensive that the other players will ask them to do magic between hands.

Actually all such complications can be avoided, and very satisfactorily. Indeed, there is a good reason why magicians should seek the card table rather than shun it as a field for prestidigitorial activity. Some of the very finest and most bewildering feats of card magic are specially suited for the card table; in fact, can best be performed there.

Which brings up another question: Why don't magicians do those tricks at the card table?

The answer is that they have ignored those very tricks. There is a fallacy prevalent among magicians that "dealing" or "counting" tricks are too slow or complicated and therefore will not hold the interest of an audience. This can prove true when performing before a large group of people, particularly if many of them are unfamiliar with playing cards. But at a card party the magician is catering to a gathering already interested in cards and their propensities; hence he should proceed accordingly.

Dealing and counting tricks are at a premium when performing at the card table. The spectators do not regard such processes as lengthy, or they would not be habitual card players. Moreover they all know how to shuffle and deal, which speeds the operation and adds the feature of audience participation which leads to convincing magic.

So in this section dealing tricks are emphasized, though the performer can intersperse them with other card tricks. Some very fine and novel effects will be explained to the reader and after he has mastered them there is no reason why they should not be included in a more general program of card magic not restricted to the card table.

In such instances, the magician should make sure that his audience likes card tricks and that the group is not too large. He can then provide his own setting by using a card table— or something similar—and inviting the group to gather round. It will be found that this intimate type of presentation will be more impressive than magic performed at longer range.

The Even Heap

As an introductory trick or an interlude between more serious demonstrations, this is a very effective item. Though it should never be repeated immediately, if people remember and ask for it on another occasion you can always oblige them, as they will have forgotten its details. Those details however are important from your standpoint, as they are why the trick really works itself.

THE EFFECT

The performer lays three heaps of cards face down. He writes something on a slip of paper and hands it to a person, telling him to hold it. He then tells the person to count the heaps from left to right: "One, two, three." After that, the spectator is asked to take whichever heap he wants and open the paper.

The choice is made, the paper opened. The message reads: "You will take the *even* heap." To the spectator's surprise, he finds that he has done exactly that, though he had free choice of the heap.

THE METHOD

From the description of the effect, the reader may gather that the spectator took the middle heap, since it would fulfill the prediction. The performer having referred to the heaps as "one, two, three," the middle heap would be the only even one.

That is true, so far as enumeration is concerned, and it applies if the spectator takes the middle heap. But there are other factors that make the prediction apply to the end heaps also.

The heaps are composed of the following cards:

Left: four cards, all spot cards with *odd* values, namely: three, five, seven, nine.

Center: three cards, all face or picture cards.

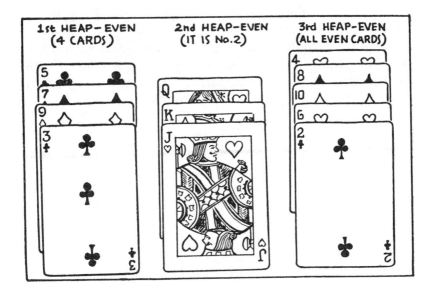

Right: five cards, all spot cards with *even* values, namely: two, four, six, eight, ten.

If the spectator takes the left heap, it is counted to show it has an *even number* of cards, whereas the other heaps when counted prove to be odd. Therefore the *even heap* was chosen.

If the center heap is taken, it is immediately termed the middle heap, since it was counted as "Two" before it was selected.

If the right heap is chosen, it is shown to contain *even*

valued cards, whereas the other heaps consist of odds or face cards.

PRESENTATION

Proper emphasis sells this trick. Should the middle heap be taken, the performer promptly declares: "You took heap two, the only even heap, since one and three are odd." He is stating this while the spectator is opening the slip of paper and the trick is done.

With either of the other heaps, the performer should immediately drop any mention of the original enumeration which, after all, was not important at that stage. He tells the spectator to count the cards in his chosen heap if the one on the left is taken. The performer then says: "An *even* number; now count the others and you will find them odd."

The performer of course can count those heaps himself, slowly and emphatically. In any case, he should see to it that all the cards remain face down.

When the spectator takes the heap on the right, the performer tells him to look at the faces of the cards, saying: "You will find you have the *even* heap, in fact you have *all* the even cards. Just look at these and make sure!"

With that, the performer turns up the other two heaps and spreads them to show that there isn't an even card among them.

The Card That Finds Itself

Finding a selected card after it has been shuffled in the pack is a basic feat of card magic. It presents a problem to the impromptu or amateur magician because, no matter how many methods he has learned, persons frequently challenge him to let them do all the handling of the pack before he tries to find the chosen card.

This would seem impossible with a borrowed pack, for it would practically amount to the card discovering itself. Yet this feat of almost automatic wizardry can be accomplished by the simple yet convincing process herewith disclosed. The only proviso on the performer's part is that the spectator follow the instructions exactly as given.

THE EFFECT

A spectator is told to shuffle a pack of cards as thoroughly as he desires, and then cut the cards into three heaps of approximately equal size, letting them lie side by side upon the table. Next he is told to look at the top card of any heap, without showing it to the performer, and let the card remain face down on that heap.

The performer then instructs the spectator to turn the other two heaps *face up* and place the chosen heap *face down* on one such heap. Then the spectator is to place the other *face-up* heap on top of all. In brief, the chosen heap, with its selected card on top, is sandwiched *face down* between two *face-up* heaps.

Now the spectator is told to cut the pack in half and shuffle the halves together in the familiar riffle or dove-tail fashion, which mixes the face-up cards with the face-down. To confuse the performer further the spectator may cut the pack, completing the cut. In fact he may repeat this cutting process several times, so that no one can even guess the probable position of the chosen card.

Nevertheless, when the magician takes the pack he has only to spread the cards from hand to hand, running casually through the entire pack. Out of the jumble he draws a card and places it face down on the table. The spectator names the card he took and the performer tells him to turn up the isolated card. It proves to be the one selected!

THE METHOD

As stated previously, this discovery is practically automatic. Follow the exact directions and you will learn the reason why.

1. DECK IS CUT INTO 3 PILES TOP CARD OF ANY PILE IS NOTED

2. OTHER 2 PILES ARE TURNED FACE UP

3. PACK WITH KNOWN CARD

4. RIFFLE SHUFFLE

5. FIRST DOWN CARD AFTER A LONG FACE UP RUN IS THE CHOSEN CARD.

The peculiar method of shuffling a pack, wherein the center section is sandwiched face down between two face-up packets, will cause a long "run" or procession of face-up cards somewhere in the pack. The face-down card immediately following this face-up run will be the selected card.

The magician has simply to pick out that card and reveal it. Cutting the pack after the shuffle does not alter this situation, provided each cut is completed. However, it may divide the long run of face-up cards so that some are on the top of the pack and the rest on the bottom. The performer must watch for this as he spreads through the pack and if it occurs he knows that the first face-down card below the top of the pack is the chosen one. This merely means that the pack must be gone through twice, which does not at all detract from the mystery.

PRESENTATION

Care must be given to the details of this trick in order to avoid any mischance that might spoil the result. Be sure to emphasize "three *equal* heaps" when the pack is first divided. Insist that it be "cut in *half*" and given a "good *thorough* shuffle, riffle fashion." If you see that the spectator is a poor shuffler, take the pack yourself and give it a dovetail shuffle emphasizing that the shuffle is thorough; then let him cut the pack.

In the case of a highly skeptical spectator you may allow him to spread the pack himself, after he has shuffled and cut it. Tell him to keep looking for his card and of course he will not find it, since the pack is face down. But you can calmly pick it out and hand it to him, when you spot it at the end of the long run.

Another way of concluding the trick is to spread through the pack, telling a person to watch for his card, but saying nothing. Note where the selected card lies; then turn the pack over and spread through it again so the person can see the rest of the cards. Knowing about where the card is, you can easily identify it when you see it face up, just ahead of a long run of face-down cards.

That enables you to lay the pack aside and tell the person to concentrate on the selected card, after which you name it aloud as though you learned it mentally.

The Honest Gambler

Card tricks with a story are always good entertainment and particularly those that have to do with gamblers. People are much interested in learning how gamblers deal themselves good hands and it is proper policy for magicians to expose the methods of card sharpers. But when an explanation can be turned into a baffling mystery, the result is all the better, and this story of the Honest Gambler fills that qualification to perfection!

Offering to show how gamblers work, the magician runs through the pack and finds the four kings, which he lays aside as he shuffles the pack. He then places the four kings on the bottom of the pack, stating that this is the way gamblers add them to a shuffled deck, the next operation being for the gambler to deal them from the bottom whenever he comes to his own hand.

So the magician deals five poker hands, but with every fifth card he deliberately draws one from the bottom, so that his hand receives the four kings. Of course the last card in the magician's hand of five can be dealt from the top. Turning up the five hands one by one, the magician shows them to be poor, average or even good—as the case may be—but his hand, the final one, is of course the winner with its four kings.

Tossing the odd hands back on the pack, the magician again puts the four kings on the bottom. He states that he will show what happened to the honest gambler who resisted the temptation of dealing himself four kings, partly because the other players were watching him too closely.

69

"On the first round," the magician relates, "the gambler actually dealt himself a card from the top, because he still had four chances to give himself the necessary kings from the bottom." During this speech, the magician deals five cards, each as the beginning of the hand; then proceeds: "On the second round the gambler became a trifle worried, so he dealt himself another card from the top, realizing that with three kings to go, he still had a strong chance of a winning hand."

Here the performer again deals a card from the top instead of a king from the bottom. He continues thus, stating:

"On the third round, his conscience really bothered him and he felt that to give himself three kings would hardly be fair. So he dealt another from the top, deciding that after all a pair of kings would serve as openers and therefore would be enough. But on the fourth round, he felt that people might even be suspicious of the openers so he dealt another from the top. Since one king was useless in itself, on the final round the gambler simply completed a legitimate deal from the top."

With the cards now dealt, the magician begins turning up the hands, to show what they contain. When he comes to the gambler's hand, he pauses as he picks it up, and states:

"You see, the gambler could easily have won with those four kings, but being honest, he didn't want them. And what was the reward of his honesty? Why, something even better." Here the magician turns over the cards and spreads them dramatically on the table. "Four aces!"

The Method

Despite the remarkable result, this trick requires no skill whatever. The dealing of four aces in the final hand, instead of the kings, will prove amazing to the spectators, but it is practically automatic. This is because the performer actually sets up the four aces before he begins the first deal.

In looking through the pack to find the kings, the performer keeps the faces toward himself. He states that he is looking for the kings, but he also weeds the aces, gathering them into a little packet with the kings. However, each king is put at the *back* of the cluster, each ace at the *front*. The bunch is removed, the pack is turned face down in the left hand and the clump of eight cards is dropped face down upon it.

1. STARTING SET-UP

2. FOUR KINGS GO ON BOTTOM

3. USE TOP CARD OF EACH HAND AS SCOOP TO TURN CARDS FACE UP — LEAVING IN POSITION

4. SET-UP FOR FINAL DEAL

4 KINGS AGAIN ON BOTTOM

The performer then states that, having gathered four kings, the gambler always removes them from the pack so it can be shuffled. Here the performer draws off the four top cards, turns them face up, and lays them aside. In shuffling the pack, the performer uses a "dove-tail" or "riffle" shuffle, where the pack is divided and the ends of each half are sprung or interlaced together. During this shuffle, the top cards of the upper half (namely the four aces) are retarded so they fall last. Thus they retain their position on top of the pack.

The four kings are then placed on the bottom of the pack and the performer deals five hands, openly drawing a card from the bottom of the pack, each time he comes to the final hand. The spectators know this, but what they do not know is that the bottom card of the first four hands is an ace. In turning up those first four hands, the performer takes the top card of the heap, slides it below and under the remaining four and uses it like a lever, to turn the whole group face up.

Thus in spreading each hand, the performer can keep the ace covered by what is now the fronting card. It does not matter if an ace is glimpsed, but the less the aces are noticed, the better. The performer simply spreads each hand casually to show that it is comparatively valueless, and he drops each of these losing hands upon the one before it, then turns up the four kings.

Gathering the four other hands, they are placed face down on the pack itself. Then the odd card in the gambler's hand is dropped on top too. After that, the four kings are placed on the bottom of the pack and the performer proceeds by dealing the second round and telling the story that goes with it.

Nobody will suspect that in gathering four odd hands, the performer was placing four aces so that they would automatically deal into the fifth hand on the next round, but that is exactly what was done. Try the trick and you will find that you receive four aces on that final deal and watch the amazement that comes over your audience!

The Triple Climax

Piling up one surprise after another, all in a single trick, is the best of magic because it catches an audience completely off balance and increases the effect proportionately. The following card experiment fulfills such specifications, as it builds up to a triple climax, with a surprising sequel, after the trick itself has reached what would ordinarily seem a satisfactory conclusion.

THE EFFECT

The magician hands a pack of cards to a spectator and asks him to mentally select any number between ten and twenty —that is, more than ten but less than twenty—and count off that many cards one by one, while the magician turns away.

That done, the person is requested to add the figures of his chosen number—for example, the digits one and seven if he took seventeen—and count that many cards onto the table from his little packet. Again he is to count them one by one, to make sure of the exact number.

Thus there are three heaps of cards upon the table: the tiny final batch; the packet from which that little group was counted; and of course the remainder of the pack, which is still larger. The magician tells the spectator to glance at the top card of the tiny group, leaving it where it is; then drop the other packet on it. Together, these are then to be placed on top of the pack.

Taking the pack, the magician riffles its end and senses the name of the card seen, stating it aloud: "ace of spades." The surprised spectator admits this is correct and thinks the trick is over. Instead, the triple climax is just about to begin!

To prove how easily he guessed the card, the magician deals three cards from the top of the pack into a little heap, face down, spelling: "A-C-E." He deals another heap to the right, a card for every letter, as he spells "S-P-A-D-E-S." Turning up the *next* card, the magician shows it to be the chosen ace of spades!

Of course it *had* to be the ace of spades, because when the magician turns up the three cards he first dealt and spreads them to show the faces, they prove to be the other three aces! To top that climax with another, he turns over the cards he used in spelling "spades" and every one of those cards proves to be a spade!

That should top everything, but it doesn't quite. Spreading the batch of spades, the magician observes that for some singular reason they run in order, from the two up to the seven. Since such an example calls for more magic of the same sort, the magician riffles the pack and blandly spells "S-P-A-D-E-S" again, dealing a card for each letter, but this time dropping them face up. Those six cards prove to be the remaining spades, in rotation from the eight up to the king!

THE METHOD

This trick calls for a set-up, or "stack" of the top sixteen cards. That is no disadvantage, because the result is so puzzling—due to a subtle preliminary feature—that the spectators either do not suspect a set-up or can not figure how one could function. Since the arrangement itself is comparatively simple, the pack is quite easily fixed beforehand, and if an extra pack is handy—as is common at most card tables —it can be set in readiness.

The arrangement is as follows: Remove all the spades and the three odd aces. Then put them on top of the deck in the following order, counting upward: king, queen, jack, ten, nine, eight, ace of spades, three aces (in any order), seven, six, five, four, three, two.

In dealing, the cards are always laid face down (until the sequel) and the ace of spades will always be the chosen card. The reason: the peculiar method of counting first a number, then its digits in reverse, invariably comes out the same.

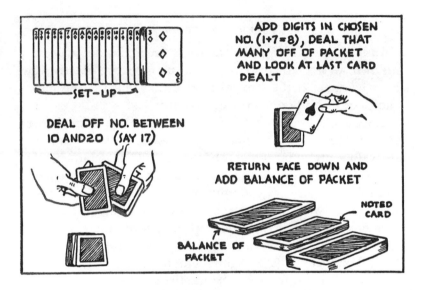

ADD DIGITS IN CHOSEN NO. (1+7=8), DEAL THAT MANY OFF OF PACKET AND LOOK AT LAST CARD DEALT

SET-UP

DEAL OFF NO. BETWEEN 10 AND 20 (SAY 17)

RETURN FACE DOWN AND ADD BALANCE OF PACKET

NOTED CARD

BALANCE OF PACKET

Because of this subtle device, you know that the spectator will arrive at the ace of spades regardless of his number.

As an example, he counts off seventeen, dealing each card on the one before. Seven and one make eight, so he deals off eight from the packet in the same fashion. The top card of the smaller group will be the ace of spades. If he had taken fifteen he would have dealt off two less, but since one and five make only six (two less than eight), he will hit the same card.

Hence the whole effect is automatic, provided the cards are dealt exactly as described, both by the spectator and the performer.   Remember that the cards must be dealt face down, always one by one, with each card going on the card just dealt. This is important in order that they come out exactly right. In adding the sequel wherein he deals spades from eight up to king, the performer deals the cards face up for the first time.   This, of course, is after he has turned up the other cards.

PRESENTATION

Instead of arranging a handy pack, the performer may carry his own, all set.   In any case, he must emphasize exactly what is to be done, at the same time insisting that the spectator's choice of a number be entirely his own.

It is a good plan to have a given number of cards—say twelve—on top of the stacked group.   The performer can then do a preliminary demonstration with this bunch.   He would say: "I want you to think of a number between ten and twenty; then deal off your number, like this."

Dealing twelve, without counting them aloud, the performer's next move is to pick up the packet and say: "After that, add the digits of your number and whatever their total is, deal off that many."   Again demonstrating what he means, he deals off about five cards beside the twelve.

Telling the spectator that he will instruct him what to do from then on, the performer simply gathers those extra cards and tucks them beneath the pack which he hands to the spectator.   This preliminary insures a correct deal by the spectator and also gives the idea that the pack itself is being mixed.

The trick may be varied by using hearts as the magic suits instead of spades; but only those two suits will work with this arrangement.

Just One Chance

This title is justified because the magician gives himself "just one chance" at finding a chosen card over which he has no control. The trick itself is most astounding, yet can be presented under the most stringent conditions. Requiring absolutely no skill, it is one of the best of all tricks in the "take-a-card" category, yet even this too-familiar slogan is eliminated by the subtle way in which the effect is handled.

The Effect

Turning away from a table, the magician instructs a spectator to shuffle his own pack—or any other—and place a spot card face up on the table before him. The person is to note the value of that card and deal two piles of cards face down, each equal to that number. That is, if the spectator turns up an eight, he is to deal two face-down heaps of eight cards each, placing these heaps to left and right of his face-up card.

Telling the person to remember both the value and suit of the face-up card—say the eight of spades—the magician instructs him to turn it face down and deal nine additional cards upon it, all face down. The rest of the pack is then to be set aside. After that, the spectator is told to gather the three heaps he has dealt and shuffle all their cards as much as he wishes.

Now for the first time the performer faces the table. He asks for the batch of cards in which the one of the spectator's choice has been so hopelessly shuffled. Running through the cards, the performer promptly discovers the chosen card—in this case the eight of spades—and reveals it the moment the spectator names it!

THE METHOD

The primary clue to the selected card is a factor that the audience invariably overlooks—the total number of the cards that are dealt. When the performer looks through that batch of cards, he first counts them to himself, while pretending only to be seeking the chosen card itself.

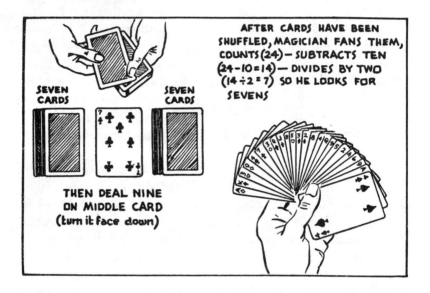

SEVEN CARDS   SEVEN CARDS

THEN DEAL NINE ON MIDDLE CARD (turn it face down)

AFTER CARDS HAVE BEEN SHUFFLED, MAGICIAN FANS THEM, COUNTS (24) – SUBTRACTS TEN (24-10=14) – DIVIDES BY TWO (14÷2=7) SO HE LOOKS FOR SEVENS

Whatever the total, the performer subtracts ten and divides by two, thus gaining the *value* of the card. As an example: with the eight of spades, there would be twenty-six cards in all. Deducting ten leaves sixteen; half of that is eight.

Knowing the value of the card—in this case an eight—the performer glances through the group to find how many cards of that value are present. If he finds only one, he simply removes it and tosses it face down on the table, telling the spectator to name his card. Once named, the card is turned up.

Should there be *two* cards of that value, the magician moves

onc to thc top of the packet, the other to the bottom.   He
then lays the packet on the table and calls upon the spectator
to name the card he took.   When the card is named, the
magician either turns up the top card, or turns up the whole
packet to show the bottom card.

With *three* cards of the chosen value, the magician places
one on top, one on the bottom, and sets the third at the card's

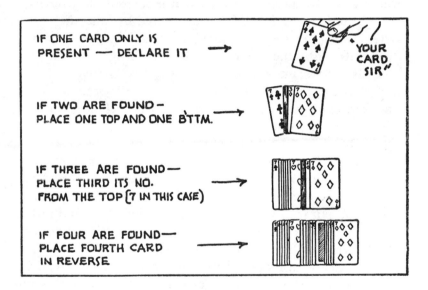

IF ONE CARD ONLY IS
PRESENT — DECLARE IT   →
                                        YOUR
                                        CARD
                                        SIR"

IF TWO ARE FOUND –
PLACE ONE TOP AND ONE B'TTM.   →

IF THREE ARE FOUND—
PLACE THIRD ITS NO.   →
FROM THE TOP [7 IN THIS CASE]

IF FOUR ARE FOUND—
PLACE FOURTH CARD   →
IN REVERSE

own number from the top of the pack.   That is, a third eight
would be placed eight cards down.   According to the suit
named, the performer shows the top or bottom card should
either be named; but in the case of the third choice, he counts
down to the value and turns up the card at that position.

Should all *four* cards of the chosen value be present, the
magician swings away long enough to plant the fourth choice
face up in the packet just below the center.   The other
choices are treated as previously described; but should the
fourth choice be called, the magician spreads the packet face

down along the table and the chosen card is seen face up, as though it were the performer's one and only choice.

PRESENTATION

Much of the presentation is covered in the handling of the various possibilities that may occur.   In any event, the performer should reveal the right card boldly and immediately, which gives the impression that such is the only way he even thought of showing it.   This is facilitated by following a key system with the various suits; for instance spades, hearts, diamonds, clubs, the order customary in bridge.

Thus, where more than one possibility is involved, the first choice (top card) would be spades; the second choice (bottom card) would be hearts; the third choice (card at value number) would be diamonds; and the fourth choice (turned-up card) would be clubs.

All are subtle, because the showing of either the top or bottom card is always natural; also, in this trick, a count down to the value (third choice) is quite logical, since the spectator himself began with such a count; while the final—and rather rare—equivoke of revealing a face-up card is always enough of a surprise to stand on its own merit.

This trick is easily tested in order to gain familiarity with its operation.   Always the performer should avoid any action that would lead the audience to believe he is counting the cards.   They should be spread slowly, as if each card were being separately scrutinized, some more than others.   The last few cards can be counted without even running through them.

There is no need to hurry, since the spectators realize all along that it is a patent impossibility for the magician to know the name or position of the chosen card in a packet so thoroughly shuffled, and the performer himself should emphasize that factor.

All this not only hides the actual subterfuges, but proves the worth of the magician's rule of not telling an audience what he intends to do until he does it. In this trick he tells them part of his intention, but not all; and the untold portion —the manner in which he will disclose the selected card— is the final touch that makes the mystery.

AFTER-DINNER
MAGIC

AFTER-DINNER
MAGIC

HERE is a type of magic that is not only popular but becomes a necessity to the amateur magician once his friends spread the news that he has taken up the art. People are more apt to request a few tricks at the dinner table than at any other place, and to refuse or beg off would be most damaging to any magician's reputation.

The Great Herrmann raised after-dinner magic to an art in itself by tossing oranges, wine glasses, and even teeming coffee cups into the air, only to have them evaporate before the astonished onlookers. The precedent thus established by Herrmann led to the development of many dinner-table tricks of a less spectacular but nevertheless intriguing variety.

Feats of after-dinner magic should normally be performed with objects found on the table, though there are certain tricks with other common items, particularly the type that can be borrowed, which are quite suited to the close range and exacting conditions of the dinner table. Many of these are simple to perform, yet difficult to detect, which is why they have been chosen for this section.

There is a distinct relation between close-up magic and dinner-table magic. Often, certain tricks found in one of these divisions might also be classified in the other. But there are also differences between these two branches of legerdemain which the magician must recognize from the outset.

At the dinner table, tricks should tend more to the sheer impromptu. Furthermore, the magician should remember that he is working as the center of a group, rather than for one person or from person to person as often is the case with close-up wizardry. As the center of the group, he is also under an occasional handicap because of persons at his very elbows.

This produces bad angles that could otherwise be avoided; furthermore, the magician is in a seated position and therefore unable to move about, or indulge in the gestures which are helpful in certain tricks. To keep taking items from his pockets or to put them away there is out of keeping with the situation and therefore apt to excite suspicion, particularly when the performer is actually disposing of some object which may have disappeared shortly before.

On the other hand, after-dinner magic has liberal compensations to the magician's advantage. He can perform certain tricks which would not be appropriate—nor even possible—elsewhere. It is even easier to drop objects into the lap or on the floor beneath the table than to pocket them, though of course this must be done with a reasonable amount of finesse.

As an example of the difference between magic of the close-up and dinner-table varieties, we may compare such items as a handkerchief and a napkin. There are some excellent close-up tricks requiring a handkerchief, but at the dinner table it is more logical to use a napkin, since it is a handy object.

However, some of the neatest handkerchief tricks, particularly those involving knots, are not adaptable to napkins, which are of thicker material and therefore too cumbersome. Offsetting this is the fact that napkins are opaque, thus hiding objects better than handkerchiefs; and they will also hold their shape to some degree, which is helpful.

Other distinctions will become obvious as the reader proceeds with his practice of after-dinner magic. The all-inclusive factor, however, is this: tricks presented at the dinner table should be somewhat incidental, rather than part of a complete or routine performance. One or two may be shown casually, then another may be recalled and performed as if on the spur of the moment.

Should the spectators want to see more magic, the performer can agree to do some after they leave the dinner table. If the group wishes to remain there, but turn over the whole occasion to magic, the performer can introduce tricks of other types that are suitable for showing at a table. This would specifically include card tricks of the sort described in the section on card-table magic, along with some close-up magic effects.

But is is unwise to exhaust a whole repertoire of dinner-table magic at one sitting, since the tricks are individual items which do not build to a climax, while the similarity of conditions—and to some degree the objects used—may cause interest to wane if the performance is prolonged.

Count the Sugar

This is one of those little perplexities that seems more a puzzle than a trick, yet can often be built into a real baffler. While it is here described as performed with lumps of sugar, other small objects, such as matches, may be used instead.

THE EFFECT

Three lumps of sugar are counted in a very curious fashion. Picking them up one at a time, the performer counts "One— two—three—" then, laying them down singly, continues "Four—five—six." He picks up one, counting "seven," another for "eight," and then pushes the remaining lump aside. Immediately he lays down the two lumps from his hand, counting "nine—ten."

All very fair and open, rather easy to follow, although done fairly rapidly. But the perplexity commences when the performer hands the three sugar lumps to a spectator and suggests: "You try it. Start counting them right here."

The curious count just won't work where the spectator is concerned and often a group of people will find themselves baffled, even though the performer demonstrates the count two or three times.

THE METHOD

The trick count will always work if started with the lumps lying on the table, which is the way the magician does it. But when the count is tried beginning with the lumps in the hand, it won't work out. Since the performer picks up the lumps and hands them to the spectator, the latter naturally begins with the lumps in hand and therefore botches the count.

PRESENTATION

In demonstrating the count, the performer should operate rather rapidly, repeating this demonstration only at intervals and then but rarely. The whole trick is to get the victim

off to a wrong start, without actually telling him to begin with the lumps in hand.

Placing the lumps in the spectator's hand is one step. The other is to point to the table when you say "Count them right here." Every time a person fails, pick up any lumps that are on the table, put them in his hand and say "Try it again," or give all the lumps to another victim saying "Suppose you try it—go ahead and count them—" again with a gesture to the table.

Sometimes a person gets it right by accident. If so, congratulate him, hand him the lumps and suggest that he do it again.   Often this will result in new failure.   If someone really catches on, tell him just to watch the others and see how they make out.   As long as one or more persons remain baffled, the trick provides good entertainment.

Three Tricky Tumblers

Though not a newcomer, this trick is comparatively little known and therefore will often prove a novelty, particularly with the added feature that makes it really baffling. It is especially appropriate as an after-dinner stunt and serves as an excellent introduction to more ambitious feats of dinner-table magic.

THE EFFECT

Three glasses are set on the table, forming a row. The tumbler in the center is upright, the others are inverted. Taking two tumblers at a time, the performer turns them both over, counting "one." Changing his hands to two other tumblers he turns them both over, counting "two." Another switch of hands so each grips a different tumbler and the performer makes another double turnover with the count of "three."

At the finish, the tumblers are all upright.

Now this proves particularly tricky, even when done slowly, because of the special provision that the hands must always turn two *different* tumblers; that is, they must each switch to another glass, before the next turn.

This necessitates the crossing of the hands at one stage of the operation, so if people find it difficult to follow, the performer can demonstrate it again.

Then the spectators try it.

Their trouble is they just can't work it. No matter how closely they follow the three moves, the majority of people will still fail and for a reason which they do not suspect at all.

THE METHOD

A simple system is as follows:

Use the hands normally to turn over the left and center tumblers.

Cross the hands and turn over the two end tumblers for the second move.

Bring the hands back to normal and turn over the left and center tumblers. This third move brings all three up.

Fairly difficult to follow unless repeated several times, this process will give the average spectator considerable trouble, but there is another factor that renders the victim's failure absolute.

After bringing the tumblers up, invert the center one and tell somebody to try the three moves, remembering that he must always change both hands to another glass. He may have followed your shifts; nevertheless, he will fail.

The reason is that you begin with the center tumbler up, the other two inverted; but in setting them for the spectator, you turn the center tumbler down, leaving the other two up. It is then impossible to bring up all three tumblers in three moves.

PRESENTATION

The "change hands" rule with emphasis on the crossing keeps most minds on the moves, not on the original arrangement of the glasses.   After showing the stunt correctly, you have only to invert the center tumbler, a very natural move, in order to let someone else try—and fail.

Furthermore, most people working from the wrong start finish with the three tumblers inverted.   Whenever that happens, you can give another demonstration by merely turning up the center tumbler before you start.   This is so similar to fixing the tumblers the wrong way that the difference is seldom noticed.

Your own system can be varied by crossing the hands at the start to turn over the left and center tumblers; bringing them to normal in turning over the end ones; crossing the hands again to turn over the left and center.

Other variations are easily learned through experiment and serve to make the "tricky tumblers" trickier than ever.   It is a good plan to swing to another trick before any spectators begin to catch on to this puzzler, but if they do catch on, it does not matter, as this is more a stunt than a mystery and should be presented in such light.

Find the Blue

Here is an ideal dinner-table mystery, utilizing the most natural of objects, three paper napkins. Though all the napkins must be identical in size and texture, one should differ in pattern or design from the other two.

For convenience, we will consider that one napkin bears blue printing; the other two red. Thus they can be described as "blue" and "reds," but this is quite optional. Any differing design or color will do for the odd or "blue" napkin.

If only plain napkins are available, one can be dotted with a blue pencil or little splotches of ink from a fountain pen, to distinguish it from the undecorated pair which represents the "reds" when the trick is performed.

THE EFFECT

Three napkins are placed on the table in slightly overlapping fashion on the diagonal. The steps should be outward, that is, away from the performer, the top napkin being the one most advanced.

One napkin has a blue design, the other two red. The magician calls attention to the position of the blue napkin, which we will assume is on the bottom. He then rolls the napkins forward, rather loosely until they form a single bundle. He then asks where the blue napkin is and is told it is on the bottom.

But when the napkins are unrolled, back toward the performer, and are lifted one by one, the blue napkin has somehow found its way between the reds. The rolling is repeated and always the blue napkin changes its position, much to the mystification of the observers.

The Method

Roll the napkins normally until near the finish. At that point, the corners originally toward you begin to come flipping over and forward. Being stepped, they flip one by one. Allow two of them to go by but stop rolling before the third does its flip.

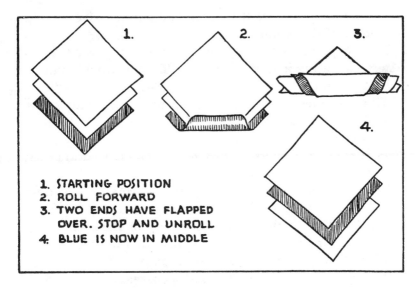

1. STARTING POSITION
2. ROLL FORWARD
3. TWO ENDS HAVE FLAPPED OVER. STOP AND UNROLL
4. BLUE IS NOW IN MIDDLE

When the napkins are unrolled, the position of the blue will be changed from bottom to center. Should you start with the blue in the center, it will unroll on top. Beginning with the blue on top, it will arrive at the bottom when the three napkins are unrolled as a unit.

Presentation

It is best to begin with the blue on the bottom. After it arrives in the middle, transfer it to the bottom and repeat. Hold the audience to the notion that the blue must always arrive in the center.

This can be emphasized by finally leaving it in the center; then roll the napkins forward again and this time stop before any ends flip or else allow all three to go. When unrolled, the blue napkin will still be in the center, apparently proving the claim that it always arrives there.

Leaving the blue in the center, do another forward roll, this time resorting to the special flip of two corners. This time the blue proves itself independent, for it arrives on top instead of in the middle.

If the napkins are rolled with the blue on top, the two-flip system will bring it to the bottom, adding another riddle to the general problem.

All these rules may be put in strict reverse by letting only a single corner ride by. In brief, you can make the blue napkin arrive anywhere you choose. Thus the trick may be elaborated into a guessing match wherein the customer is always wrong.

When the magician rolls the napkins forward and says "find the blue" he pauses while he allows two guesses to be made. Then, letting one, two, three (or none) of the corners flip over, he can unroll the napkins to prove that the blue always arrives where nobody thinks it will.

The napkins start with forward steps (about an inch is satisfactory) and when unrolled still hold that same relation. However, it is good policy to lay the napkins rather irregularly, so that any slight deviations from the diagonal will not be noticed.

Through the Table

Driving one solid object—such as a glass of water—through another solid object—such as a dinner table—is a favorite pastime with capable magicians, though not without certain difficulties. Here, however, is a novel version of such a mystery, which provides simplified operation along with increased effect.

The Effect

Lifting the table cloth, the magician places a glass of water beneath it and holds the glass through the cloth. Having set the glass nicely in place on the table top, he strikes it downward. The glass goes right through the table and the wizard brings it from beneath.

The Method

The magician is provided with a disk which is the approximate size of a glass-top. This disk can be cut from stout cardboard or made by cutting the rim from the thin metal top of a preserve jar. The disk is previously—and secretly—slipped beneath the table cloth.

Lifting the table cloth with one hand, the magician takes the glass in his other hand to place it beneath the cloth. However, by lifting the cloth rather high, he is able to carry the glass beneath the table without that fact being detected. Here he places the glass—which should be but partly filled with water—between his knees, leaving it gripped there.

The hidden hand, now free, slides beneath the lifted table cloth and picks up the disk. It raises the disk and the other hand grips it through the cloth. The disk should be kept high enough to simulate the glass of water.

Giving the disk a slight lift, the hand suddenly releases it and the other hand simultaneously delivers a sharp downward stroke as though driving the glass through the table. The free hand goes beneath the table and brings out the glass of water.

PRESENTATION

It is important that this trick should be shown only when the performer is at the end of the table or so seated that none of the spectators can gain a view from the side. Often he can place himself so that he can perform the trick, otherwise he should reserve this effect for another occasion.

By punching a tiny hole in the disk, a strong white thread may be attached. This thread should run over the edge of the table so that later, by drawing upon it, the performer can reclaim the disk. An excellent cover for this maneuver is to have a napkin lying by.   In gathering up the napkin the thread can be drawn beneath it and the disk drawn free under the napkin folds.

Should a large napkin or small cloth be available, the performer can use it instead of the regular table cloth, or can perform the trick on an otherwise bare table.   In this case the disk is secreted beneath the outspread napkin.   Afterward, the disk can be drawn away by its thread or can be gathered up in the folds of the cloth.   Drawing it away is sometimes preferable, as the disk can be dropped in the lap while the napkin is casually spread, folded, and laid aside.

There is a very neat bit of business which may be introduced when the magician becomes familiar with this trick, particularly in connection with a rather large glass.   Holding the disk higher than the glass-top would normally be, the magician leans forward, stating that he will test the solidity of the table.   This enables him to reach his free hand beneath the table and take the glass from between his knees.

Holding the disk through the cloth, the magician pushes it slightly downward as though hitting the bottom of the glass against the top of the table.   At the same time his other hand thumps the top of the glass upward against the table.   The muffled thumps sound exactly as though the glass were under the table cloth.   This preliminary illusion adds greatly to the subsequent effect of the glass apparently penetrating the table.

The Match Twister

Dinner-table tricks often demand repetition and this one is particularly suited to such treatment. It should be repeated in order to produce its full effect, since one success could readily be charged to luck. But when a trick never fails, there must be something to it. And that is true with this match mystery.

THE EFFECT

Taking three matches of the large, blue-tip variety, the performer marks one with a lead pencil so it can be distinguished from the other two. He tosses the three matches across the table and asks someone to dip them out of sight. This done, the person passes one of the three matches to the performer beneath the table.

Without bringing the match into sight, the performer announces whether it is the marked one or not. He then brings the match up from his side of the table and shows that he is correct. Apparently the performer has distinguished the pencil mark by sense of touch, but other people find it quite impossible to do so.

Time and again the trick is repeated, becoming more and more mystifying as it proceeds, since the performer names the marked match without fail, distinguishing the plain ones with equal facility.

THE METHOD

This really is a twister. The marked match is prepared in a manner that no one ever suspects. Grip the ends of the match firmly and twist it back and forth, weakening the fibers. This makes no change in the appearance of the match, but from then on it will have a "give'" which the other matches lack.

Receiving a match beneath the table, the performer has only to take it by the ends and twist them slightly in opposite directions. If the match yields in pliable fashion it is the marked one; otherwise it is ordinary.

PRESENTATION

It is a good plan to have some matches handy, among them a weakened one which can be already marked. However, if matches must be borrowed, there is a simple way of fixing the marked one without anyone knowing it.

Mark a match and ask someone to pass it beneath the table, or simply put your hands beneath with the match. Pretending to tell if you can feel the pencil mark, give the match the strong twist treatment that makes it pliable. Bring it out, toss it to a spectator, and try two plain matches beneath the table, but of course do nothing to them.

Everything is then ready for the "match twister" to be demonstrated in its usual style.

String a Ring

This is essentially an after-dinner trick because it must be performed upon a table, and a dinner table is as good as any other. The required items are a piece of string, a safety pin, a finger ring—which may be borrowed—and finally a handkerchief, although at the dinner table a napkin can conveniently serve in that capacity.

The Effect

A finger ring is placed on the table, and beside it a safety pin. A piece of string about two feet in length is stretched so that the ring and pin are close to its middle. A handkerchief is laid over these, leaving the ends of the string in sight.

That calls for magic, so the performer promises some. Reaching beneath the handkerchief, he states that he will put the ring on the string, using the pin to hold it there. After a brief manipulation, unseen under the cloth, the magician tells a spectator to take the right end of the string and pull it out.

This is done and as the string emerges from beneath the handkerchief, the ring is seen on the middle of the string, genuinely there, with the string passing through it, the safety pin clamped alongside. The pin is opened and removed, so that everyone can examine the ring and the string and marvel at this accomplishment.

The Method

Under the handkerchief, take a loop of string and push it through the center of the ring. Then open the safety pin and fasten it so that it includes two portions of the string:

the right sector of the loop, and the string proper that is located to the right of the ring.

Place your left forefinger in the loop.   Bring your right hand from beneath the handkerchief and gesture for someone to take the right end of the string and draw upon it, or, if the company proves timid, pull the string yourself.   In either

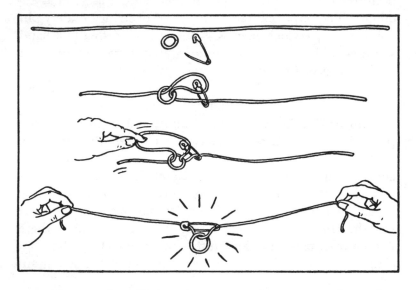

case, the result will be the same.   Out comes the string, ringed and pinned in the middle.

All provided that you keep your left forefinger in that precious loop!   What happens—as you can see by testing this without the covering cloth—is that the left end of the string comes hustling through the ring as fast as the latter travels to the right.   What is more, you can speed this process by moving your left forefinger—and its loop—toward the left.

Urge that the string be drawn rather rapidly to the right, or perform that service yourself.   Then there is no worry about anyone noticing the left end of the string as it disappears briefly beneath the handkerchief. The ring and its clamping safety pin come into sight so soon that they capture all attention.

The purpose of the safety pin is to act as a drag that prevents the ring from sliding back along the string. Nobody knows what happens beneath the handkerchief and the peculiar position of the pin adds to the mystery at the finish.

The Dissolving Coin

Here is a way of vanishing a borrowed coin from an ordinary glass of water, with an added and convincing feature that makes it seem as though the coin actually dissolved itself in the liquid.

THE EFFECT

Taking a small drinking glass, the performer pours about an inch of water in it and sets the glass on his left hand.   Borrowing a coin, he has someone place it in the center of a handkerchief or napkin; gripping the coin through the cloth, the magician holds it above the glass and drops it.

People hear the coin fall in the glass; not only that, the magician lifts the cloth and shows the coin there.   He covers the glass again and a few moments later whisks the cloth away.   The coin has dissolved and both the glass and the cloth may be inspected.

THE METHOD

In covering the glass the first time, the performer tilts it by raising his fingers upward.   This is not seen beneath the cloth.   The coin is held above the tilted outside of the glass; when it is dropped, the coin strikes the outside and slides or falls to the curve of the fingers.

The clinky sound gives a perfect illusion of the coin landing in the glass, but that is not all.   Bringing his hand level, the magician grips the glass through the cloth and slides the glass over the coin.   The coin may be shown, apparently in the glass, by lifting the cloth and allowing a straight downward look.

The refraction of the water causes the illusion of the coin being on the bottom of the glass instead of beneath it. The glass is again covered with the cloth and lifted away, leaving the coin in the magician's hand which keeps it hidden in the bend of the fingers.

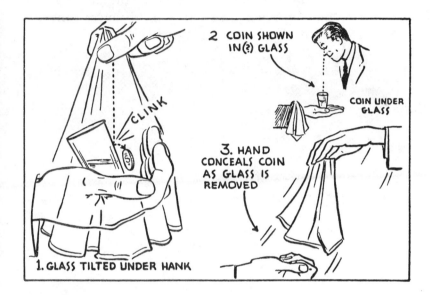

PRESENTATION

A large coin—a quarter or even a half dollar—is the best to use. The bottom of the glass should be larger than the coin, but the glass itself should be a comparatively small one, giving the hand plenty of space to receive the coin.

When the glass is slid over the coin any clinking sounds are natural, as they could occur while the coin is in the glass A good pretext for lifting the cloth to show the coin actually "in the glass" is to decide that some more water may be needed. In fact, the magician may pour in a little more after he lifts the cloth.

A neat way to dispose of the coin is to state that the cloth must be made air-tight. Gripping the glass through the cloth with his upper hand, the performer reaches to his pocket with his lower hand, carrying the concealed coin and dropping it there. He brings out a rubber band (previously put in the pocket) and fixes it around the rim of the glass, tightening the cloth. In due course the coin "dissolves" and the cloth is removed, the elastic coming with it.

Dime, Wool, and Match Box

By far the most spectacular of all devices for reproducing a borrowed coin after vanishing it, this was long a closely guarded secret. Performed in an elaborate style, it remained a really remarkable mystery until it was reduced to lesser versions that lacked the strength of the original effect. Properly treated, however, the trick can be as effective as ever, even when simplified.

Its correct adaptation as a pocket mystery suitable for dinner-table presentation is therefore given here. As an item of close-up magic it will prove equally mysterious.

The Effect

A borrowed dime is marked, preferably with a corner from a gummed label, which a spectator can initial in pencil. The dime is placed beneath a handkerchief and the spectator is given a closed match box. The dime vanishes from the handkerchief, the match box is opened and inside is found a small but well-rolled ball of wool. The wool is unwound and inside it is found the very dime that disappeared.

The Method

A special appliance is required in the form of a flat metal slide about two inches long and large enough to allow a dime (or penny) to slip through it. Since the slide can be open at one side, it is very simply made by bending a piece of thin metal into the correct shape. Or a metal tube, such as an aluminum cigar holder, may be flattened and cut to the right length.

A length of thin wool is wound around the end of this slide

and the winding is continued in criss-cross or V-fashion so that the wool covers the mouth of the tube and comes up on each side. A rubber band, twisted double, is used to hold the wool firmly in place.

The tiny ball of wool is placed in a match box, with the tube projecting from the drawer. Closed as far as possible, the match box is girded lengthwise with a double-twisted

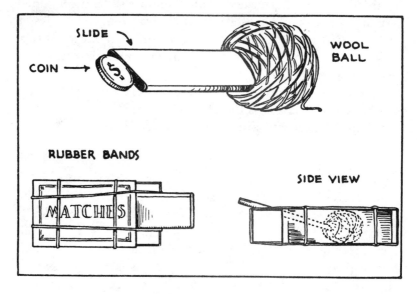

rubber band that forms a V, with its extremities pressing the sides of the tube. Another rubber band should be doubled around the match box.

This affair is in the performer's pocket. To put a borrowed coin into the ball of wool, he has only to reach in his pocket, drop the coin into the slide, then work the slide free. When the box is brought out it will be tightly closed by the rubber bands. The same will apply to the ball of wool which will show no opening whatever. Unrolled, the ball of wool disgorges the missing coin.

PRESENTATION

For the vanish, the performer should use a handkerchief with a very broad hem, which he has previously opened in order to insert a duplicate coin. When the borrowed coin is placed in this handkerchief, the performer retains it in one hand, while with the other hand he finds the hidden coin and grips it through the cloth.

This is given to a spectator to hold while the first hand goes into the pocket and drops the coin into the metal slide. If there is trouble withdrawing the slide from the box and wool, it is simply overcome. Bring the hand out and grip the tube through the pocket, from the outside. Reach over with the other hand and down into the pocket as though trying to find something. With this hand, pull the match box and its contents off the gripped tube, in a forward and downward direction, the space in the pocket being ample.

Hand the match box to the spectator and take the handkerchief. Give it a shake and it can be shown empty because the coin will slide away in the hem. The spectator may then open the match box and unroll the ball of wool himself. It is most effective to have him place the ball in a glass and keep drawing on the free end. The coin will then land in the glass with a very convincing clink.

Instead of the handkerchief vanish, the performer may employ the "dissolving coin" as previously described, but should use a smaller glass than regularly, since he is dealing with a coin of dime or penny size. In this case he will need no rubber band to place around the glass rim, as he will naturally reach into his pocket to bring out the match box.

PARTY MAGIC

PARTY MAGIC

THIS section contains full instructions for putting on a complete magic act before a sizable group of people, done entirely with apparatus and materials that can be prepared by anyone at a trifling cost. It is commonly supposed that expensive apparatus and intricate contrivances are necessary to produce a magic show that will entertain a full-fledged audience, but those which are included here will prove quite as effective as some of the most elaborate effects.

Many professional magicians utilize tricks of the sort described here, intermingling them among others that require special tables, cabinets and the like. Some very showy tricks, large enough for a whole audience to appreciate, are found in such a category. So a special group of such mysteries has been devised or gathered in order that a full quota of them can be made into a show all its own.

Party magic seems an appropriate term for tricks of this order, because they are doubly suited for presentation at a party. First, they are good enough and big enough for the occasion; again, the fact that the appliances are fairly ordinary is an advantage because the spectators can not find anything wrong with them.

Many aspiring magicians have made the mistake of bringing a whole array of velvet-draped tables and chromium-plated apparatus to a party, only to find that their friends question such paraphernalia and therefore the show becomes difficult instead of easy. As a result the store tricks get packed away in a closet and the magician resorts to devices of a less suspicious nature. That is the expensive way as well as the wrong way to become a magician, and if readers of this book have not already tried it, they will save themselves an unnecessary investment by following the procedure recommended here.

Try the tricks described in this section and after you have picked the ones you like best, arrange them for your act. If you wish, you can dress up some of the appliances, for instance, where large paper balls are mentioned, you can use fancy pincushions instead.

Pack all such apparatus in a small satchel or brief case and, if you want, add a fancy cloth or drape to your baggage so that you can place it over a table and thus dress up the act.

In presenting magic at a party, there is an important point to remember, namely, that your audience is apt to be at bad angles. In fact, sometimes people may be behind you, which will ruin certain types of tricks. In preparing this section, allowance has been made for this, hence you will find most of the tricks here described to be of the "all-around" variety, where angles do not matter.

When angles do matter, one way to counteract them is to pick the right spot in the room from which to work. This is either at the end of the room where there are no doorways or mirrors, or better still, in a convenient corner, where mirrors do not matter if present because their reflection will be at an angle away from the spectators.

All this is good procedure in itself and therefore worthy

of mention even when not needed; but the chances are that the reader will find it of value after he has progressed still further in magic and decides to add some special props to his equipment. Many of the tricks supplied by magic dealers can be worked into a demonstration of party magic provided good judgment is shown in their selection and they are not added until the performer has gained some experience in this type of entertainment.

The chief idea is that a party show, particularly among friends, should never be top-heavy with specially made equipment. Even if people are baffled by the performer's handling of such apparatus, they will be inclined to credit the appliances with having produced the deception, rather than the performer. There should always be something of the informal, an impression of the unprepared, in the mysteries that compose a party show. Once the magician has established such a *cordiale* with his audience, he can safely introduce a piece of special equipment and expect his audience to accept it with due appreciation of his own ability.

Party magic will put life into any party, provided it is well presented. During preliminary rehearsal the performer should play to an imaginary audience, timing his actions and adding patter or talk to accompany the presentation. In giving the actual show, the performer should remember that he is acting the part of a magician and try to add an air of mystery to his work. Just how far this should be carried depends of course upon the individual.

A performer can be his natural self, yet at the same time adopt a manner that lends itself to mystery. Inasmuch as the audience is being mystified meanwhile, this can really prove impressive What must be curbed is the tendency to overdo it, a fault too common with beginners. By keeping the mysterious within the limits of the natural manner, rather than assuming a false personality, the correct result will be gained.

Homing Colors

The appliances used in this trick are inexpensive, easily obtainable and simple to prepare; yet they produce a result as effective as many costlier gadgets regularly merchandised as magical equipment.

The required items are two small glass tubes, some strips of red and blue paper, also a double-ended pencil which has lead of those two colors. The strips of paper are cut to form colored bands that gird the glass tubes. All these articles can be purchased at drug stores or stationery shops.

THE EFFECT

Two glass tubes are shown, each girdled by a strip or band of colored paper: one red, the other blue. Two slips of white paper are given to different persons, along with a red-and-blue pencil. One person writes his name in red, the other in blue. The papers are rolled tightly and each is inserted in a glass tube.

The performer emphasizes that the paper with the *red* message is placed in the tube with the *blue* band and vice versa. That is, the papers are put in the *wrong tubes* from the standpoint of their corresponding colors. Giving the tubes to two spectators to hold, the magician commands the papers to transpose themselves to the proper tubes.

Although the tubes and their contents have not for one instant left the sight of the audience, this amazing result occurs. When the papers are taken from the tubes, the red message is discovered in the red-banded tube, the blue message is in the blue-banded tube.

THE METHOD

The trick is accomplished with the aid of two loose, slightly oversized bands that slide on and off the glass tubes. First gird the tubes with narrow bands, which are glued in place. Then make the extra or special bands, simply pasting them to form loose loops.

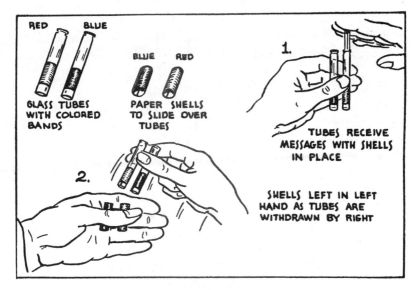

This fit should be fairly snug, enough so for the outer bands to remain in place when they cover the solid bands. The red outer band or "shell" covers the solid blue band; the blue shell goes over the solid red.

The paper used should be colored on one side only, so the difference will not be observed by anyone who gains a slanted view through the glass. Since the shells are put on beforehand, the performer introduces the glass tubes as just the opposite of what they really are, so far as colors are concerned.

Thus when the red and blue messages are rolled and thrust into the "wrong" tubes, they are actually going into the proper ones, provided the performer can dispose of the shell bands. He does this easily and indetectably by placing them in the left hand with the bands concealed by the fingers and the thumb pressing the inner side of the bands. The right hand then draws the tubes straight upward and thus leaves the shell bands in the left.

Thus the tubes, not the messages, are the objects transposed, and the spectators, being unaware of this, are convinced that the messages somehow changed places, after the tubes are opened and their colors checked.

PRESENTATION

Though simple of operation, this effect requires careful presentation. The first stages should be performed deliberately, calling full attention to the fact that the messages are placed in tubes of opposite colors. Next, when the tubes are taken in the left hand, they should be shown all about, before the left hand is swung back toward the right.

This causes observers to forget whether the "red" tube or the "blue" is on the right or left, particularly as the left thumb drapes itself across the bands. The right hand, when it draws the tubes upward from the left, should immediately go into a sweeping gesture of its own, before passing the tubes to two spectators.

With attention on the right hand and the tubes, the left can easily dispose of the shell bands which it retains. One system is for the left hand to dip into a pocket, leaving the bands there, and pretending to bring out an "invisible powder" which the magician says he will sprinkle on the red message. The right hand then goes into its pocket and pretends to bring out some "invisible powder" for the blue.

Another system is for the right hand to take the pencil after passing out the tubes. The right transfers the pencil to the left hand, which immediately puts it into the inside coat pocket, letting the shell bands drop with it. During this casual action, the right hand is pointing from one tube to the other, as the performer states he will cause a transmigration of colors.

Whichever procedure is used, final emphasis should be given to the forthcoming transposition as though nothing at all had happened up to this point and that the really magicial task still lies ahead.

Sticky Water

Tricks that apparently defy some natural law are always very effective and therefore suited for presentation before a large group of spectators. This one nullifies the law of gravity and, because of the size of the objects used, it is excellent for a demonstration of party magic.

The Effect

The magician shows a soda bottle half filled with water. He pours a small quantity of the water into a pitcher which is on the table; then, deciding that he has just the right amount, he sets the first two fingers of his left hand over the opening of the bottle and inverts it with his right.

Some water trickles from between the magician's fingers down into the pitcher, over which he holds the bottle. But when he spreads his fingers and draws them away, the water remains in the bottle as though glued there!

The magician can approach the spectators with the inverted bottle and its mysteriously suspended contents, but for the climax he holds the bottle above the pitcher; then, with his free left fist, gives the bottom of the bottle a solid thump. Instantly the spell is broken and the blow punches the water out of the bottle down into the pitcher.

The bottle may then be examined, yielding no clue to the mysterious force that retained the liquid while the bottle was upside down.

The Method

A special but easily prepared appliance accounts for the mystery. Cut a disk of cellophane, just the size of the mouth of the bottle, from the wrapper of a cigarette package or some similar item. The disk does not have to be cut perfectly, but the closer it is to the right size and shape, the better.

Have the disk lying handy beside the bottle or pitcher. Either the disk should be moistened, or the fingers of the left hand can be dampened when you first pour some water from

the bottle. The fingers then pick up the disk simply by pressing against it.

The bottle is held upright and the left fingers contact the top, pressing the disk against it. When the right hand inverts the bottle, some of the liquid will trickle out at the edges but by slowly and carefully spreading the fingers the edges of the disk will seal themselves against the lip of the bottle mouth and adhere there, holding the water in place.

Now the bottle can be shown at quite close range, the cellophane being invisible against the water. For the finish, the mere act of jolting the bottle with the free fist will literally punch out the water so it pours down into the pitcher carrying the cellophane disk with it, unnoticed.

PRESENTATION

There are a few special pointers that may prove helpful with this trick.   First, it is often possible to place the disk on the left fingers in advance, in which case no pick-up of the disk is necessary.

Furthermore, the left hand may be shown rather freely, even when the disk is on the fingers, because the cellophane can not be seen there, unless it is brought too closely into the light.

Don't worry about anyone seeing the disk after it falls into the pitcher of water.   You will have enough trouble yourself in locating it later on.   Nevertheless, for close-up work, there is a variant to the finish which is sometimes useful.

Instead of punching out the water, use a pencil to poke up in the bottle and "loosen" the water, as you can term it. Simply press the pencil to one side and the water will gush out past it while the pencil flattens the disk against the inner neck of the bottle, where the piece of cellophane will remain unnoticed after the pencil is withdrawn.

The Baffled Farmer

Two hats and seven paper balls are the only items required for this rather elaborate and convincing demonstration of a clever magical story. Best of all, it can be performed without any special skill; hence all the emphasis is on proper presentation. This point is important, for though the method is simple, the routine should be rehearsed, as it depends upon an ease and surety of operation that misleads the spectators.

THE EFFECT

Showing two empty hats, the magician states that they represent a pair of barns situated near a farmhouse. He places the hats upon the table, crowns down; then exhibits a pair of paper balls, wadded from newspaper or tissue paper. He drops one paper ball in each hat, stating that each represents a thief, hiding in that particular barn.

Next, the magician displays five more paper balls which he sets in the space between the hats. These five represent sheep that the thieves intend to steal by first coaxing into the barns. One thief captures the first sheep, the other the second, and so on, the performer illustrating this by picking up the "sheep" one by one and dropping them alternately into the hats.

Hearing the farmer coming, the thieves decide to release the sheep. So the magician demonstrates this part of the story by replacing the five paper balls on the table, one from one hat, one from the other hat, and so on. However, finding that it was a false alarm, the thieves steal the sheep again, the performer picking up the five balls one by one and dropping them alternately into the hats as before.

Now, according to the story, the farmer really arrives, bringing the sheriff. They call upon the thieves to come out of the barns, bringing the sheep with them. Somehow, the two thieves have managed to get into one barn all alone, while the five sheep have magically assembled in the other.

For when the performer picks up the hat on the left, he

DIAGRAM OF PROCEDURE

takes from it the two paper balls representing the thieves, while, when he turns over the hat on the right, out roll the five balls that stand for the sheep!

THE METHOD

The whole trick depends upon a bold but baffling subterfuge introduced during the course of the story. Though the performer terms two of the paper balls "thieves" and the other five "sheep," actually all are *identical*, and therefore one type can pass for the other at the finish. Though some persons will doubtless recognize this, there is still another factor that baffles them, namely why there should only be two paper balls in one hat and five in the other, when the distribution seemed equal.

It's all done in the pick-up and replacement. In picking up the "sheep" one by one, the performer drops them in the hats as follows: Right, left, right, left, right. In replacing five paper balls upon the table, he takes them from the hats in the opposite rotation, that is: Left, right, left, right, left.

At this point the spectators assume that there is one ball (a thief) in each hat, whereas the hat on the left is actually empty and that on the right contains two paper balls.

In picking up the five again, the performer assigns them to the hats as he did before: Right, left, right, left, right. This seems to distribute them in the original fashion, but there are now two (the thieves) in the hat on the left and five (the sheep) in the hat on the right, so everything is ready for the climax.

PRESENTATION

As the presentation of this trick depends chiefly upon the story, you should rehearse the patter with the routine. While it is best to tell the story in your own style, it should follow the general "patter line" given below, the words in italics representing the various actions. Start by placing the two hats on the table, then put two paper balls at the left and five at the right. Take your position behind the table so you can demonstrate the trick in open, effective fashion.

"This is the story of Farmer Brown and his adventure with the two thieves. To begin with, Farmer Brown was very lucky, because he had two barns, but he was also unlucky because both barns were empty." *Pick up hats, show them, and replace them.* "So one night, along came two thieves."

Pick up two paper balls from left.   "Finding two empty barns, each took a private barn for the night."   *Drop the paper balls into the separate hats.*

"Now Farmer Brown had a flock of five sheep that liked to graze between the barns."   *Pick up five paper balls from right and drop them one by one between the hats.*   "Noticing the five sheep, the thieves began to call them into the barns: first one into this barn; then one over here; one over here; one over here—and one over here."

Pick up the five balls one by one and drop them right, left, right, left, right into the hats.   Then pause and gesture with both hands, one at each hat.

"Having thus divided the sheep, the thieves were suddenly alarmed to hear the farmer leaving the house.   So they quickly let the sheep go, just as they had taken them.   One from here—"   *take a ball from hat on left*   "—and from here—"   *take a ball from hat on right*   "—and from this barn, that barn, and this barn."   *Remove three more balls, left, right, left, with each word "barn."*

"But the farmer went away, so the thieves took back the sheep, just as before: one—two—three—four—five."   *With each number pick up a ball, right, left, right, left, right, and drop it in the corresponding hat.*   "Only you can imagine their chagrin when they saw that the farmer had returned, bringing the sheriff with him.   That was when the two thieves did some very quick thinking.

"And that's also where the magic comes into this story. When the farmer and the sheriff looked into the barn on the left, did they find a thief with half a flock of sheep?   Not at all!   What they found—"   *tilt hat and lift out two paper balls, dropping them back in again*   "—were the two thieves, all alone, and sound asleep, while over here in the other barn—"   *tilt hat on right and let the five paper balls roll out*   "—were all five sheep, safe and sound.

"It seems impossible, but that's what happened. How it happened we'll never know, because the thieves are asleep and can't tell us and the sheep can't talk. As for the farmer and the sheriff, I can assure you they are quite as mystified as we are!"

Sawing Through a Rope

Though the implement used for this singular penetration effect is a borrowed handkerchief and not a buzz saw, the title is deserved, because there is a distinct illusion of one object being sawed through another. It is an excellent trick to show to an informal group, for while the objects are large enough for all to see, the mystery can be accomplished in the very midst of the spectators.

The Effect

A borrowed handkerchief is tied around the middle of a piece of rope, or heavy cord, the ends of which are held by two spectators. Taking the ends of the tied handkerchief, the magician gives it a sawing motion back and forth along the rope. Quite amazingly, the handkerchief comes clear of the rope and is given for examination, knot and all, while the rope itself proves to be quite ordinary and utterly unchanged by this penetration of one solid through another.

Like the handkerchief, the rope or cord may be borrowed, provided it is three feet or more in length. The handkerchief is genuinely tied, which gives this mystery a very convincing effect.

The Method

The result depends upon the type of knot used and its position on the rope. Therefore it is best for the performer to tie the knot himself, rather than make adjustments later.

Facing the rope, you hang the handkerchief over it, the long end at the back. With your right hand, bring that long end forward beneath the rope and place it across in front of the short end from right to left.   Form the knot by pushing the long end under the short end from left to right.

Pull the tip of the long end downward in front of the rope and leave the knot quite loose.   Now if you observe the handkerchief closely, you will discover that it is *still* hanging over the rope with a short end down in front, the only difference being that the long end has been loosely tied around the short.

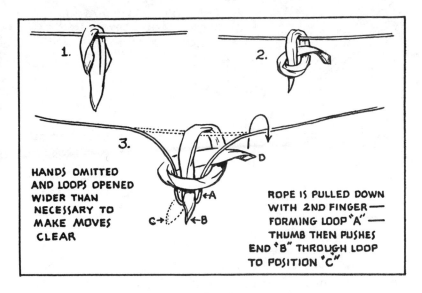

1.

2.

3.

HANDS OMITTED
AND LOOPS OPENED
WIDER THAN
NECESSARY TO
MAKE MOVES
CLEAR

C→   ←B

←A

D

ROPE IS PULLED DOWN
WITH 2ND FINGER —
FORMING LOOP "A" —
THUMB THEN PUSHES
END "B" THROUGH LOOP
TO POSITION "C"

Now if you grip the short end with your left hand, thumb at the front, fingers at the back, all pointing upward, you will find that you can work your middle finger up through the loose knot until it reaches the rope.   At this point you tell the spectators to loosen the rope; as they do, you hook the rope with your finger and draw a center loop down through the knot.   You then push the end of the rope through the loop with your left thumb and when you have the spectators draw the rope tight, the handkerchief will be off the rope.

This process is clearly shown in the illustrations, but should be tested with a rope or string, which can be stretched on a table or tied between two chairs, in order to acquire the exact maneuver.   So much for the mechanics of the trick; the rest depends upon the presentation which follows.

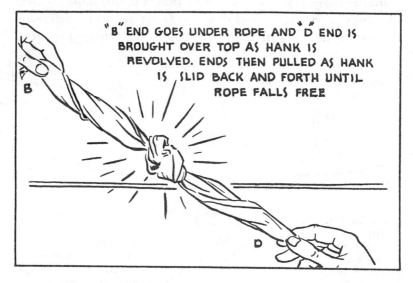

"B" END GOES UNDER ROPE AND "D" END IS BROUGHT OVER TOP AS HANK IS REVOLVED. ENDS THEN PULLED AS HANK IS SLID BACK AND FORTH UNTIL ROPE FALLS FREE

PRESENTATION

The whole trick should be handled deliberately, as it requires care more than actual skill.   Draw the looped string just far enough to push the end of the handkerchief through and immediately tell the persons holding the end of the rope to draw it tight.   All the while, the right hand should be holding the other end of the handkerchief, and when the rope is tight, the hands draw the knot tighter as they move the handkerchief back and forth along the rope and then lift the handkerchief free.

To make the maneuver completely deceptive, the handkerchief should be *turned over* as you push the short end through the loop of rope.   Turn it from right to left; that is, push the short end downward and toward the back with the left hand, while the right hand brings its end upward and over toward the front.

The knot is then under the handkerchief and you can calmly change hands from one end to the other in the act of drawing the knot tighter. Nobody will suspect that the handkerchief is actually off the rope, so you should lay great emphasis on the sawing motion which finally results in the handkerchief coming upward and free.

Remember again: care, not skill, is the essential. The fact that a handkerchief can be removed from a rope while knotted there is something of a riddle in itself. The fact that you do not loosen the knot, but tighten it instead, will cause people to suppose that the handkerchief *must* be on the rope until the very finish.

By operating deliberately and giving the handkerchief the turnover, you can hide the whole process with the loop of rope. White rope of a soft variety is preferable and the same applies to cord, provided of course that the handkerchief is of the common white variety. This will minimize the chances of anyone observing the brief manipulation with the loop.

The Weird Tube

Though strictly impromptu in appearance, this mystery meets the specifications of those requiring fancy apparatus. In a sense it is an apparatus trick in disguise, which makes it all the better, since the spectators will not anticipate the startling result. Specially suited to a performance of party magic, the weird tube will fit in any program; but it can also be shown at close range—even at the dinner table—if due care is taken to meet the existing conditions.

THE EFFECT

The performer shows a paper tube, some eight to nine inches long and two-and-a-half to three inches in diameter. The tube is made of ordinary typing paper and is fastened together with paper clips. Showing the tube empty, the magician starts to push a pencil through it, only to find that the pencil is not long enough, so he has a better idea.

Taking a handkerchief, the performer drapes it loosely over one hand and holds the tube in front of it with the other, so that people can look through and sight the approximate center of the handkerchief. The performer then lays the handkerchief on a book or plate and folds the corners of the cloth into the center. He does this with one hand, because the other is holding the tube, which the performer promptly sets on the center of the handkerchief.

Now it is quite possible to drop the pencil into the tube, but there is something else that is equally easy. Taking a glass of water, the magician calmly pours its contents down into the tube. Why worry about the book or whatever is underneath? The folded handkerchief should absorb the water readily enough. Of course that might be asking too much of the handkerchief. The best thing to hold water is a glass. So the magician snaps his fingers above the tube, lifts it, and there the amazed spectators see a glass, somehow arrived from nowhere, containing the water which was so recently poured!

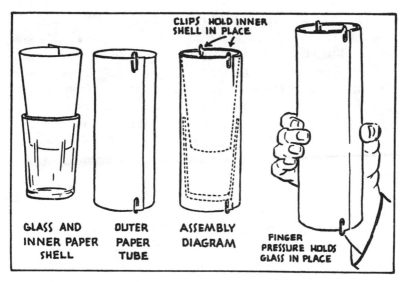

GLASS AND INNER PAPER SHELL

OUTER PAPER TUBE

ASSEMBLY DIAGRAM

CLIPS HOLD INNER SHELL IN PLACE

FINGER PRESSURE HOLDS GLASS IN PLACE

THE METHOD

The tube is specially prepared beforehand, but in a very simple way. First take the glass which is to appear, making sure you have one with a very clear bottom, and shape a paper tube around it. With the average glass, a thick sheet of typing paper will suffice, the width of the paper representing the height of the tube.

Now take another sheet of paper and fit it inside the glass. This inner tube should taper gradually, so if the glass itself slants slightly inward, so much the better. However, a straight-walled glass will generally prove satisfactory. Cut this inner tube three or three-and-a-half inches short at its narrow end. Fasten it with paper clips and insert it in the top of the cylindrical outer tube, clamping the two edges with the clips.

The glass may then be pushed in from the other end of the double tube and will nest neatly between the outer cylinder and the slanting inner lining. Adjustments can be made to conform the double cylinder to the glass. Looking through the tube from the top, which is to be the front end, the interior will appear empty if not scrutinized too closely.

The slant of the lining makes the inner tube appear to be the outer in perspective. The fact that it is from a third to a half shorter goes with the illusion. The bottom of the glass is transparent, hence observers will see clear through it. This is why a plain-bottomed glass should be used, but any slight wavers will not be noticeable if the performer pays due heed during the presentation. Any paper clips used to fasten the short end of the inner tube will be mistaken for those which clamp the bottom edge of the outer cylinder.

Have the trick cylinder lying on the table. Pick it up and casually show the interior from the front end, start to insert a pencil, then lay it aside. Pick up a handkerchief, spread it loosely behind the tube and let people sight through. All during this process the glass is in the tube, pushed well forward—or upward—so only its invisible bottom is in the path of vision.

Lay the handkerchief on the book and tilt the tube with its bottom downward. Fold the corners of the cloth into the center, set the tube on the handkerchief and release pressure of thumb and fingers so that the glass will slide slowly downward, the folded cloth deadening its arrival. Instead of dropping the pencil into the tube, pour water from another glass. Then lift away the double tube and show the glass that arrived within.

Since the inner tube is short, it does not interfere with the water, as the glass has slid down below the short end of the lining. It is a good idea to pour water from a smaller glass, which is filled to the brim. Then the mysterious glass that arrived from nowhere will be about two-thirds filled and will make a good show in comparison to the smaller glass that was laid aside.

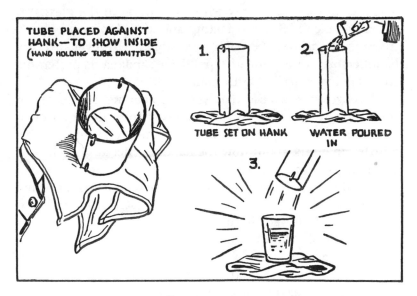

TUBE PLACED AGAINST HANK—TO SHOW INSIDE (HAND HOLDING TUBE OMITTED)

1. TUBE SET ON HANK

2. WATER POURED IN

3.

PRESENTATION

With a clear-bottomed glass and an average background, the tube may be shown quite freely from the front end. Otherwise, the preliminary business with the pencil should be emphasized, particularly when showing the tube at close range. At the dinner table, a knife or spoon can be used instead of a pencil.

What the performer does is this: keeping the tube slightly in motion as he shows it empty, he picks up the pencil and starts to push it into the tube. That enables him to hold the tube still because the slight motion of the pencil and the hand which guides it from the front, will confuse the observer's eye sufficiently to prevent the detection of the glass barrier which is toward the rear of the tube.

The business with the handkerchief also helps the illusion, allowing a very convincing show of the tube's interior. Being draped, the handkerchief presents an irregular surface which conforms reasonably with any wavers in the glass. A white handkerchief is satisfactory and a napkin may be used instead, if working the trick at a table. However, a fancy handkerchief, or a colorful type like a bandana, is preferable when giving a party performance.

Moreover, the excuse that you are gauging the center of the handkerchief distracts full attention from the interior of the tube. Similarly, when the water is poured into the tube, a little rapid talk about how the handkerchief absorbs it, will cover the trickling sound of the liquid arriving in the hidden glass. If people do hear the sound it does not matter, because the arrival of the glass in the tube is mysterious whether it preceded or followed the pouring of the water.

At the finish, the tube may be crumpled and pocketed or thrown away. It takes no time to make a new tube for another performance, and to treat it as valueless will allay any suspicion regarding its preparation.

For a party show, where a table may be set to avoid angles, an excellent combination effect can be worked. Have a stack of books handy and use one of the books as a resting place for the handkerchief and tube. Have another handkerchief lying on the stack of books. In pouring the water into the tube, pour it from a glass that is identical to the one that is to appear in the tube.

After pouring from this duplicate glass, step over to the stack of books, pick up the handkerchief there and drape it over the empty glass. Keep the hands low as you do this and set the empty glass behind the stack of books. Immediately bring the empty hand up beneath the cloth, pressing the tip of the forefinger against the tip of the thumb, so that they form a horizontal circle.

With the fingers below, these will form the shape of a glass as you boldly extend your hand forward. Command the glass to fly into the paper tube and capture the water already poured there. Use your free hand to whisk away the handkerchief, at the same time opening the concealed hand and turning it palm up, as though the glass had been resting on it.

Lifting the tube, you can then show glass, water and all. The tube is crumpled, tossed aside, and the handkerchiefs may be dropped behind the books where they cover the vanished glass, in case anyone should approach the table later. Afterward, the glass can be gathered with the handkerchiefs and packed away.

The Triple Knots

Here two comparatively simple but deceptive knot tricks are combined to form a really magical effect. Though each device is clever in itself, separately they are puzzling rather than mysterious; but when worked together, they gain the needed element. This use of existing methods to form a composite mystery is very valuable in magical performances and often builds trivial tricks into real marvels.

THE EFFECT

Two coils of light rope are lying on the table. The performer lifts one rope by the end, letting it stretch full length, then coils it again and places it on a chair. Uncoiling the second rope he proceeds to tie it into three knots. Holding the rope by the ends, he swings it toward the chair where the coiled rope lies.

Amazingly, the knots on the swinging rope dissolve. Tossing the rope across the back of the chair, the magician lifts the coiled rope by one end. One by one, the three knots come into view, forming a row on the rope that was so recently placed aside. Somehow, those knots have passed from one rope to the other!

THE METHOD

Discounting the magician's logic that the knots passed from rope to rope, the method cracks down to two phases: First, some secret method of making a coiled rope tie itself in knots; second, a system of tying three knots and having them literally fall apart.

First, the trick coil.

Hold the left hand palm up and lay the rope across it so that a few inches of rope project beyond the left thumb. The right hand takes the rope in similar position a few inches to the right of the left hand. The bulk of the rope is dangling beyond the right thumb.

Gripping its stretch of rope, the right hand turns over toward the left, forming a coil of rope which it places, in

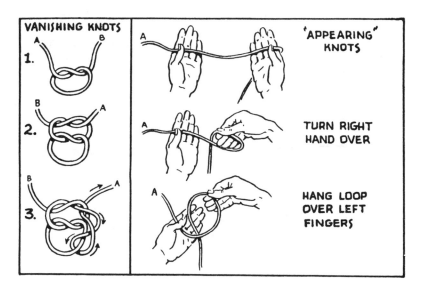

backhand style, over the left fingers and leaves there. Thus free, the right hand lifts another stretch of rope and repeats the process of looping it over the left fingers. This is done a third time, using up most of the rope, which should be about four feet long.

The right hand then takes the coiled rope from the left and in so doing, the fingers of the right hand—aided by the left if needed—press the lower or left end of the rope right through the coils, so that it emerges on top, or at the right. The rope is placed on the chair in this position.

To make knots appear on that rope as the climax of the trick, the performer has only to lift the rope by the projecting end and draw it straight upward.

Second, the vanishing knots.

Tie a single knot in the center of a rope, keeping the right end of the rope toward you as you form the knot.

Keeping that same end front (the end now being at the

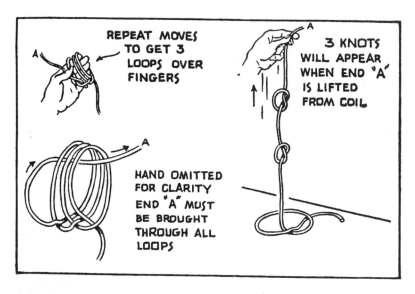

REPEAT MOVES TO GET 3 LOOPS OVER FINGERS

3 KNOTS WILL APPEAR WHEN END "A" IS LIFTED FROM COIL

HAND OMITTED FOR CLARITY END "A" MUST BE BROUGHT THROUGH ALL LOOPS

left) form a second knot above the first. This forms a square knot, but it is not drawn tight; instead, it is kept in two fair-sized loops.

Your third knot is a very special one. Take the front end of the rope (now at the right) and push it through the lower loop from front to back. Bring it around to the right and to the front again; then push it squarely through the center of the upper loop. Draw the ends of the rope slowly and this array of knots will tighten, only to unsnarl and dissolve entirely as you draw the rope taut.

PRESENTATION

The ropes are coiled at the outset so that the performer will have an excuse for coiling one again when he shows it to be ordinary and lays it aside. Of course these original coils are quite normal, being made in ordinary fashion.

Lifting one rope and showing it, the magician coils it in the special fashion described and places it on the chair. He then lifts the second rope, uncoiling it normally, and ties the trick knots that vanish, numbering the knots one, two and three as he forms them.

As the knots vanish, the magician swings the rope to the chair back with one hand and lifts the coiled rope with the other. Thanks to the previous use of ordinary coils, the slow appearance of the knots, one by one, will have a really startling effect. A slight wiggling of the rope not only enhances the mystery but aids the arrival of the knots.

Double Double

Tricks with rope have become so popular in recent years that it would be quite possible to give an entire performance with magic of this variety and monotonous indeed it would be. What rope magic needs is something both different and direct. As far as feasible, "double double" provides these elements, and it will prove a startling effect for any occasion, though it is specially suited to party magic because of the slight arrangement necessary.

The Effect

Exhibiting a rope some four or five feet long, the magician holds it dangling from his left fist, with the end of the rope projecting a few inches above. About three inches below the left hand is a knot, already tied in the rope, to which the performer points with his right forefinger.

Then, taking the knot in his right hand, the magician in some mysterious fashion removes it from the rope, because it is no longer there. Before the spectators can do more than guess at the knot's disappearance, the magician makes a throwing motion with his right hand and the knot appears back on the rope.

To prove that this was something more than an optical illusion, the magician repeats the trick, snatching the knot from the rope and throwing it back in place. Whereupon, he gives the knotted rope to the audience and the knot is found to be not only genuine, but double. This, the performer explains, is because he worked the trick twice.

THE METHOD

The rope is arranged beforehand.   About ten inches from
the top end, tie a double knot and pull it tight.   Eight inches
further down, tie a slip knot.   This is done by crossing the
rope and pushing a little loop up through, pulling it just
tight enough to resemble a solid double knot, yet loose enough

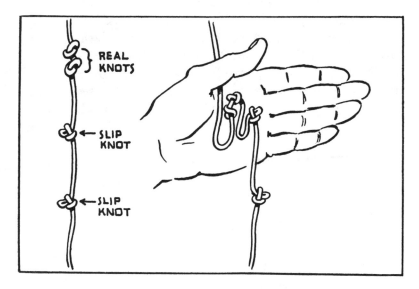

to be pushed apart.   Eight inches further down, tie another
such slip knot.

Take the rope loosely in the left fist, with about two inches
of rope showing above.   The first knot—the real one—will
be four inches below the left hand.   Lift the knot and place
it in the left hand where it is gripped in the bend of the forefinger.

This brings along some three or four inches of rope, so
that the next knot—the first false one—is about four inches
or so below the left hand.   Bring up that knot and place
it with the one already gripped in the left hand.   Now close

the left fist tightly, making sure to tuck in any stray folds of rope.

Result: the next knot—the lower false one—will be the only knot visible on the rope and will appear three or four inches below the left hand. This is the knot that you point out when you show the rope to the audience, saying that you have a rope with a knot tied on it.

Grip that knot with the right hand and push out the slip with the thumb. Pretend to carry the knot away in the closed right hand, gesturing the rope with the left. Make a throwing motion with the right hand, opening it at the same time. In doing this, bring the right hand in front of the left and downward, without touching the left hand. Simultaneously, the left hand releases its lower knot which drops, along with some extra rope, to the position at which the audience first saw a knot.

This effect is quite startling and since the rope is a long one, nobody notices that it has gained a few inches. The left hand, still fisted, now holds a solid knot, while the rope again has a slip knot on display. So the right hand has only to repeat the maneuver and with the throw the left lets the hidden knot—which is genuine and double—fall as the fake knot previously did.

Presentation

The method itself covers most points of presentation, although it should be emphasized again that this trick must be shown in magical style, rather speedily and somewhat dramatically. At the finish, the rope is handed to a spectator so that he can untie the knot and find it double; not that the rope "may be examined," which is a bad statement to make, though the case is actually so.

The only other factor in presentation is that of having the rope in readiness. It can be lying loosely, with its knots hidden beneath it, at some convenient spot where you can turn away and quickly fix it in your left hand. Or the doubled portions may be set beforehand, in which case the rope may be lying partly stretched upon the table, but with some object like a handkerchief or sheet of paper covering the doubled portion.

As the right hand lifts the hiding object to place it aside, the left picks up the rope, taking the doubled portions in the fist. With the back of the left hand toward the audience, the right can make a few adjustments as though measuring the rope. Then the left can be turned with its closed fingers toward the spectators and the trick is ready to be shown.

The Tri-cut Rope

The cutting and restoring of a rope has become such a common feat of modern magic that today a rope and pair of scissors are more symbolic of a magician's calling than a rabbit and a wand.   What is therefore needed is a rope trick that goes the average one better, both in effect and method. The "tri-cut" fulfills those qualifications.   The rope is cut into three pieces, instead of merely two, while its restoration is automatic, making this practically a self-working trick.

THE EFFECT

The magician measures a five-foot piece of rope into three lengths and ties knots to indicate the divisions, thus forming the rope into a double loop with a middle strand.   With a pair of scissors, he cuts the rope at the knots and lets it dangle, showing the three sections.   Coiling the rope around his left hand, he sprinkles some invisible powder on it; then uncoils the rope one-handed.

Not only have the knots vanished; the rope itself is restored to a single piece and can be tossed to the audience while the magician proceeds with his next marvel.

THE METHOD

Hold the rope high with the left hand, which is at the upper end.   With the right hand, grip the rope about a third of the way up, and lift the right hand to the left.   The rope is then adjusted so that the three lengths are approximately the same, the left hand holding its end, the right holding the curve of an inverted U.

The left end of the rope is tied around the portion held by

the right hand. The rope then consists of a loop and a
loose end. Tie the loose end to the center of the loop.
Next, insert the middle fingers of each hand in the two loops
thus formed, making three lines of rope, knotted at both
ends.

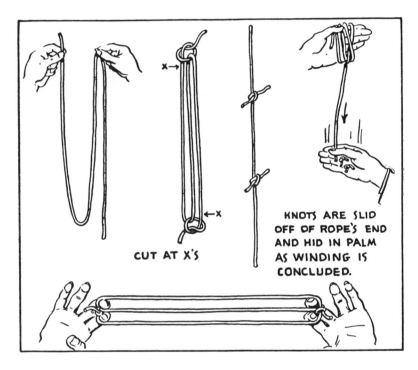

CUT AT X'S

KNOTS ARE SLID
OFF OF ROPE'S END
AND HID IN PALM
AS WINDING IS
CONCLUDED.

This gives the impression that the rope is in three sections.
Actually each knot represents an end of the rope. Lift one
knot and slide it slightly; then pick up the scissors and cut
the portion adjoining the knot. That means do *not* cut the
rope that slides through the knot.

Repeat this operation with the other knot. The result
is a length of rope with two knots showing on it, each representing one-third of a rope which is presumably cut into

three sections.   Actually, the knotted ends have been cut free, but this fact is discreetly ignored.

Grip one end of the rope in the left hand, palm toward you, and start coiling the rope around the left hand with the right.   Coming to a knot, retain it with the right, sliding it along to the next knot, which is captured and brought along in the same fashion.   The spectators think the knots are in the left hand, whereas they are in the right, which carries them off the end of the rope when the coiling is completed.

The right hand goes to the coat pocket, carrying the knots with it, the performer announcing at this point that he will "show the audience some invisible powder."   Leaving the knots in the pocket, the right hand emerges and pretends to show the powder which is "so invisible the eye can not see it." The right hand makes a pretence of sprinkling this powder on the rope, which the left hand then uncoils with a throwing motion, showing the rope entirely restored.

PRESENTATION

The trick should be presented smartly, with a running patter that should be delivered in the performer's own style. The idea is chiefly to convince the spectators that the rope has been cut in thirds and this is not difficult if the procedure is reasonably brisk.

Particular emphasis should be given to the rope when it dangles with the two knots showing, as it actually appears to be in three sections, as stated.   Keeping the rope slightly in motion at this stage is helpful, as it prevents keen eyes from analyzing the knots too closely.   During the coiling, the magician can remark that he is "rolling up the rope, knots and all" which carries the pretence even further.

Summarized, the result depends upon the individual, but in any instance, this "tri-cut rope" will make an effective finish to a series of rope tricks.   The only danger point is in the cutting of the knotted ends and even this can be avoided by a simple expedient. If trouble is anticipated, prepare for it by marking the rope with little dabs of ink, five or six inches from each end. Those markers tell which portions of the rope to cut and the trick can be done any time, anywhere, except in the dark.

The Penetrating Knot

This combination effect has been adapted especially for a program of party magic, and will prove highly effective if carefully presented. The maneuvers or manipulations it requires are easily learned, depending more on precision than skill. These moves are either hidden or can be done deliberately; therefore practice and rehearsal are the real elements necessary.

The Effect

Showing a small tray, or large book, the performer asks a person to assist him by holding that object in front of a handkerchief which the performer, in his turn, has stretched between his hands. The performer faces the audience, the assistant stands at the performer's left, facing him and extending the tray toward him.

The assistant naturally holds the tray level, so the performer asks him to tilt it forward in order to hide the center of the handkerchief. That done, he has the assistant hold the tray a little higher. The performer then can bring the ends of the handkerchief around to the front of the tray, with the bulk of the handkerchief behind—or beneath it.

Keeping the tray at that exact angle, the performer moves it in front of the assistant, who now faces the audience directly. The assistant can then grip the ends of the handkerchief, keeping them taut against the tray. His own hands free, the magician then takes another handkerchief and ties a knot in its center.

Now comes the dramatic punch.

The assistant is holding the tray so that the handkerchief behind it is vertical. Facing from the assistant's right, the performer stretches the second handkerchief vertically across the front of the tray, calling full attention to the knot in its center. When the magician gives the ends of the visible handkerchief a sharp tug, the knot instantly vanishes. Laying that handkerchief across the assistant's shoulder, the magician tells him to release the tray but retain the ends of the

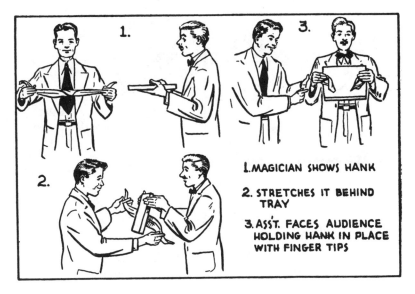

1. MAGICIAN SHOWS HANK

2. STRETCHES IT BEHIND TRAY

3. ASS'T. FACES AUDIENCE HOLDING HANK IN PLACE WITH FINGER TIPS

handkerchief that he is holding. Catching the tray, the performer whips it away.

There, in the center of the original handkerchief, is the missing knot, midway between the assistant's hands. Apparently the performer has caused it to jump from one handkerchief to the other, penetrating the tray!

THE METHOD

This effect has two stages: first, the secret tying of a knot in the original handkerchief; second, the forming of a knot that will vanish from the other handkerchief.

For the first process, place the end of a handkerchief between the first and second fingers of the left hand, but have the hand *palm up* and lay the handkerchief *over* the left forefinger so that it comes beneath the rest as it extends rightward. The left thumb must be *above* the loose left end of the handkerchief.

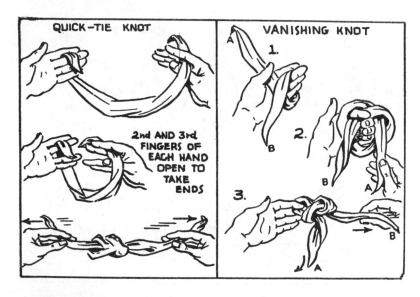

QUICK-TIE KNOT

VANISHING KNOT

1.

A

B

2.

B

B A

3.

2nd AND 3rd FINGERS OF EACH HAND OPEN TO TAKE ENDS

A

B

The right hand assumes a vertical position, clipping the right end of the handkerchief between its first and second fingers, forefinger above, second finger—and the rest—below. The right thumb is beneath the handkerchief toward the left, as the loose end of the cloth pokes out in back of the fingers.

Approach the hands, swinging the left palm down. You will find it is no trick at all to bring the loose ends of the handkerchief to a position where the right end can be gripped between the left thumb and second finger; while the right thumb and second finger can similarly grasp the right end.

When such a hold is taken, the mere act of drawing the hands apart will produce a genuine knot in the center of the handkerchief.

In brief, this is a simple way of tying a knot in the center of a handkerchief without releasing the ends, the process being a change of grip.

4. KNOTTED HANK HELD IN FRONT OF TRAY

5. MAGICIAN VANISHES KNOT BY JERKING HANK

6. TRAY IS REMOVED — KNOT HAS TRAVELLED TO HANK HELD BY ASS'T !!

Hardly a trick in itself, this maneuver is remarkably swift and certain—therefore deceptive—when properly or momentarily hidden. It must be acquired so that it can be done automatically and without hesitation. It then becomes the secret method whereby a knot is placed in the handkerchief that goes beneath, or behind, the tray.

After the tray has been tilted forward, the performer is showing the ends of the stretched handkerchief, held in the special manner described; those ends are projecting from the sides of the tray. In telling the assistant to raise the tray slightly, the performer suits words to action and lets his hands come toward each other, beneath the tray in order to give it an upward nudge.

This is when the hands tie the automatic knot by simply bringing the hands together and drawing them apart, the ends of the handkerchief immediately being drawn out beyond the edges of the tray. The action is both natural and brief; the same hands still hold the same ends of the handkerchief. Hence no one will suspect that anything special could have taken place, particularly as the performer has not yet spoken of knots at all.

Thus knotted, the handkerchief is fixed so that the assistant holds the ends clamped against the tray, everything being ready for the climax.

The second stage of the trick follows.

This consists of tying a knot visibly in another handkerchief, but it must be the sort of knot that will evaporate when the ends of the cloth are pulled. That is, it is not a knot at all, but a false knot.

There are various ways of making such trick knots, but the one to be described is probably best suited to this particular effect. It is easy, can be formed openly and deliberately, as well as being certain of final operation. The moves should be practiced, however, until they can be performed with a fair degree of speed. The less hesitation, the more convincing the action.

Hold the left hand palm upward and lay the handkerchief across it so that the center of the handkerchief dangles from the near side of the left hand. The right hand takes the near end of the handkerchief, carries it under the left hand and up between the first and second fingers of the left, drawing it fairly taut across the portion of the handkerchief resting on the left palm.

The right hand now takes the far end of the handkerchief and pushes it up through the loop in back of the left fingers.

Then, gripping that end, the right hand draws it into what seems to be a knot, the latter including the left fingers. This, however, is a false knot, and as the right hand tightens it, the third and little fingers of the left hand ease down and out, leaving only the first two fingers in the loop.

With their tips, those fingers—first and second of the left hand—retain the cloth that passed between them. The other fingers of the left hand grip the dangling portion of the handkerchief while the right hand keeps drawing its end. This produces a false knot or loop in the center of the handkerchief. It will pull loose when the ends of the handkerchief are sharply tugged.

Hence the performer has only to take the handkerchief with its apparent knot, stretch it vertically in front of the tray, and pull the ends at the right moment.

PRESENTATION

Presentation is important in this effect, so important that, once the actual moves are acquired, the rest might be termed all presentation.

The performer should state that he intends to "stretch the handkerchief beneath the tray" without mentioning what is going to happen later. He should pause to twist the handkerchief ropewise, by twirling it from the ends. Bringing the hands slightly together, he puts them beneath the tray, illustrating how he wants it "a little higher" and immediately he brings the handkerchief into sight, twisting it a little tighter as he tells the assistant to "tilt the tray forward."

That is, the performer simulates the vital maneuver which is to come later, but without forming the instantaneous knot. He reserves that important process until the tray is set so he can give it a natural nudge from beneath; and all his preliminary operation is with the purpose of making that move look natural—and therefore be unsuspected—when the right moment arrives.

Measuring the tray to make sure the ends of the handkerchief will come beyond its edges, is also part of the preliminary work. This is when the handkerchief is fairly loose; hence its ends just about come into sight. Thus when the knot is secretly formed after the handkerchief is twisted more tightly, the ends will stretch as far—or even further—giving the impression that the handkerchief must be in its original condition.

All this makes the presentation deliberate, so when the performer comes to the vital move, he does not have to hurry it. Behind and below the tilted tray, the hands perform the maneuver neatly and simply come into sight as they make the slight upward nudge. Too rapid action at this point would be a mistake; therefore the performer must guard against making the maneuver too difficult, rather than too easy.

The trick can be rehearsed with an imaginary helper, but it is better to have someone actually hold the tray. In performance, it is also good practice to use a regular assistant if available, whether or not that person acts as an actual assistant during the remainder of the program or is called upon as a member of the audience. Such a helper will follow the performer's cues or actions, thus making the presentation more effective. Nevertheless, once well rehearsed and tested with a few actual performances, it will prove quite easy to guide the actions of any co-operative person called upon to assist.

The tying of the knot in the second handkerchief should also be done deliberately, twisting the handkerchief tightly before making the false knot. Once the "knot" is tied, it should be exhibited against the background of the tray, a pause being effective at that point.

Here the performer can count to three, or call upon some

magic word to make the knot pass through the tray. Also at this juncture he should for the first time explain the actual purpose that he has in mind, namely, to pass the knot from one handkerchief to another, through an intervening object.

A sheet of cardboard, a tabloid newspaper, or a book of Atlas proportions may be used instead of a tray.

MENTAL MAGIC

MENTAL MAGIC

RATHER than a class of magic suited for certain circumstances, "mental magic" represents a distinct branch of the mystic art which, though adaptable to many conditions, demands a presentation distinctively its own.

Here the magician undertakes to deceive the mind rather than the eye and this requires special emphasis on certain phases of each trick, along with suitable discussion or patter. Moreover, the performer must adopt an attitude quite at variance with the magician's usual style.

Instead of making amazing things happen, the performer waits for them to happen of themselves. He deals in mental impressions rather than magic words. He treats curious results as expected coincidences, rather than some tribute to his skill or magical ability.

As would be expected, a line of demarcation has resulted among professional magicians where these two styles of mystery are concerned. The wizard who deals in mental effects prefers to style himself a "mentalist," letting the term "magician" apply solely to the popular conception of the performer who presents objective marvels, such as vanishing anything from coins to rabbits, or producing such items from thin air.

Occasionally a mentalist will include a few bits of old-line magic in his program; while magicians in their turn often add mental effects to their repertoire. The difference is this: the mentalist is stepping out of character when he does so; whereas the magician is not. Claiming a power of mind over mind, the mentalist becomes a show-off when he dabbles in standard magic except as a minor diversion, just as a magician would do if he interspersed his act with too many juggling feats instead of sticking to his business.

But a magician is definitely in character when he introduces mental effects in his performance. Being a magician, all wonders should come within his range. If mentalists claim that something more than mere dexterity lies behind their marvels, it is only fitting for a magician to show that he has an option on that certain power, since all things should be possible to a magician.

Since this is a book on magic, mental effects are therefore included, particularly as they represent the most modern branch of magic itself. In presenting such feats as magic, it is not necessary to tout them as anything supernormal beyond the degree of making them good entertainment.

The performer may speak of "mental coincidence," or state that he will now present a demonstration of "apparent telepathy" in which he calls upon people to "concentrate" rather than "watch closely." Yet often a good trick of mental magic may be shown blandly and at the finish the performer may act as surprised as his audience.

While the effects in this section may be presented as a full program in themselves, this would require considerable high-pressure, since they have been chosen more for their entertainment value rather than as a means of convincing the uninitiated that mental magic is something more than magic. The best plan is to intersperse them with other tricks, or to use individual mental mysteries in other types of programs.

Some will be found particularly good for close-up magic. Others involve playing cards and are therefore suitable to include with card tricks. In a performance of party magic, certain of these mental marvels will be stand-out attractions and should therefore be used in such a program, according to individual choice.

It's a Date

Mental magic with a calendar forms the theme of this intriguing trick, which offers a few variations that make it quite effective. It is performed with a monthly sheet from an ordinary calendar, and to make it more of a stunt, two or three such sheets may be given to different spectators, so that more than one person may participate.

The Effect

Using a heavy pencil, someone forms a block around nine numbers on a monthly calendar, forming a cluster of dates running three in each direction: vertically and horizontally. The person names the lowest number in the block and immediately the performer gives the total of the whole cluster. When the nine dates are added, this total proves correct.

Or someone may block nine dates, three by three, then add the total of the corner numbers. When this total is given to the performer, he asks the person then to concentrate upon the central date of the square. Promptly the performer names that number.

As a variation, a spectator may block off a square of four numbers, add them all and name the total. Then, while the spectator focusses his mind on the lowest number in the square of four, the performer visualizes and announces it.

The Method

While basically a mathematical trick, the factor of the calendar adds some puzzling angles. The systems work with any blocks of dates, regardless of the month, which simplifies it from the performer's standpoint, whereas the average spec-

tator is apt to regard the problem as complicated and therefore difficult.

To gain the total of a block of nine from the lowest number, add eight to that number and multiply by nine. This
can be done more rapidly by multiplying by ten and sub-
tracting the number multiplied.

Example: 4 plus 8 makes 12, times 9 totals 108 can also be
calculated thus: 4 plus 8 times 10 minus 12.

Given the total of the four corner numbers in a block of
nine, the central number is gained by dividing the total by
four. This works with any nine block on a monthly calendar.

To find the smallest date in a block of four, after the total
is named, simply subtract sixteen and divide by four. This
too is uniform with any such block.

PRESENTATION

The performer should stress the fact that *any* sheet may be
taken from the calendar without showing him the particular

month.   He may ask, however, whether the month has thirty or thirty-one days, as though that had something to do with the effect.   Or he may exclude February from the list until he repeats the trick—with variations—at which time he makes February allowable, just to make it harder.

Also, it is effective to insist that the various spectators concentrate on their central numbers or lowest numbers, when those are being named from the totals.   This gives the trick the status of a mental mystery rather than a mathematical stunt.

For best results, these calendar perplexities should be shown in connection with other mental mysteries, as the spectators will then be in the right mood to accept them as something more mental than mathematical.

The Telltale Card

Rather than a card trick, this rates as a mental mystery of the prediction type, playing cards being used because they happen to be a common and convenient item. At least that is the magician's plausible statement when he introduces this effect into a mental-magic program, where it rightfully belongs. Suitable also for a performance of party magic, this will invariably prove itself a stand-out mystery.

The Effect

Showing a pack of cards, the magician runs through the pack face up to show that all the cards are different. Turning the pack face down, he fans it or spreads it on the table and removes a card at random. Holding the card sideways with its face toward himself, the magician writes a prediction along the margin and drops the card face down in a hat.

The magician declares that his prediction is the name of another card, the very card which a spectator in his turn will take from the pack. Spreading the pack face down, or leaving it so if it is already on the table, the magician lets the spectator touch or take a card, which is promptly dropped in the hat along with the one that bears the prediction.

Here it should be noted that the face of neither card has so far been shown and that the magician insists on the spectator having an absolutely free choice of the card he takes. In fact, the spectator can switch from one card to another and may take the advice of other persons present.

It follows therefore that there is only one chance in fifty-one that the performer can have even guessed the spectator's card beforehand. But there is no guess-work to this super-mystery. Reaching into the hat, the magician removes his card, turns it face up and lets people read what he has written on the margin. There they see the name "eight of hearts." The spectator removes his own card from the hat and, to his amazement and that of the remaining witnesses, it *is* the eight of hearts!

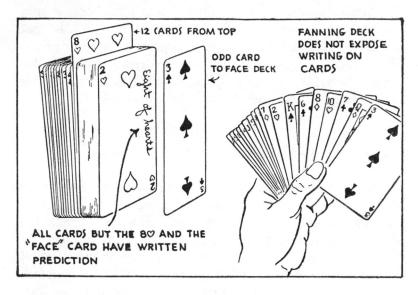

ALL CARDS BUT THE 8♡ AND THE "FACE" CARD HAVE WRITTEN PREDICTION

← 12 CARDS FROM TOP

ODD CARD TO FACE DECK ←

FANNING DECK DOES NOT EXPOSE WRITING ON CARDS

THE METHOD

Sure-fire tactics feature this near miracle. It all depends upon some neat preparation of which only the magician is aware, since he has personally provided it. The pack used is his own, a point which he treats only casually, and which seems to have no bearing since he shows the cards to be all different. But actually this is the vital factor.

The pack is prepared thus: Remove the eight of hearts and any other card. Then, along the margin of every remaining card—fifty cards in all—write the name "eight of hearts." Assemble the pack so that all the written margins are to the right. On the bottom of the pack place the odd card. Put the eight of hearts a certain number from the top, say twelve.

Now when this pack is spread face up, to show that all the cards are different, nobody sees the written margins, since the pack is normally spread from left to right. This applies if the cards are spread along the table; likewise if they are

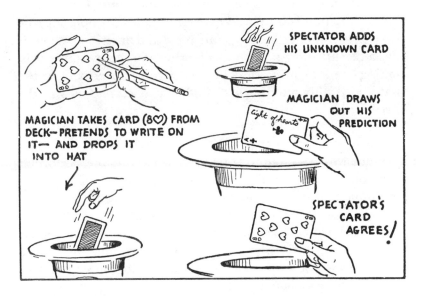

SPECTATOR ADDS HIS UNKNOWN CARD

MAGICIAN TAKES CARD (8♡) FROM DECK—PRETENDS TO WRITE ON IT— AND DROPS IT INTO HAT

MAGICIAN DRAWS OUT HIS PREDICTION

SPECTATOR'S CARD AGREES!

spread between the hands, the left thumbing them over toward the right. Everyone observes that the pack is well mixed and therefore takes it to be quite ordinary.

In spreading the pack face down and making his "random" choice, the performer actually pulls out the twelfth card— or the card at whatever position he placed the eight of hearts —or, if he prefers, he can simply fan the faces of the cards toward him and draw the eight of hearts as though it were any chance card.

The magician does not show the face of this card. He holds it toward himself and pretends to write something in pencil along its margin, then drops the card face down in the hat. Next the spectator takes a face-down card and drops it in the hat without looking at it. But whatever card he takes will already have the margin-written name of "eight of hearts," the card that the performer already placed there!

In stating that he will take his "prediction card" from the hat, the magician removes the spectator's card instead and hands it to him face up. Whatever card it is, people suppose that it is the one the magician took and inscribed, since it has a pencilled message on its margin. So the spectator, mistaking the remaining card for his own, removes it from the hat and is duly astonished to find that it corresponds to the prediction.

PRESENTATION

Since this trick requires no skill whatever, the performer can concentrate entirely on its presentation which, in turn, is simple and direct, but therefore should not be neglected. Bringing out his pack, the performer remarks that he "will use a pack which is complete and well-mixed," spreading the cards face up to justify the statement. He then announces that "this is not a card trick but a psychological experiment in the accuracy of prediction."

Declaring that he will take a card at random, the performer adds that a spectator is to do the same, with the pack face down so that his choice will in no way be influenced by the cards themselves. But first there is the matter of the prediction, so the performer pauses to "write it on the random card."

After the two cards are in the hat, there should be another pause while the magician recapitulates on what has happened, meanwhile putting the rest of the pack back in its case which, in turn, he places in his pocket. In taking the hat, the magician should hold it tilted slightly toward him as he brings out "the prediction card," which he can do quite casually as it will be above the other.

The performer should hand that card face up to one person and give the hat to another; but here he can add another subtle touch. Noting the card that bears the writing, say the king of spades, the performer can remark:

"You see my card was the king of spades, but that is unimportant. What really matters is the name of the *other* card that I wrote along the margin of the king. I want you to read it aloud, then look at *your* card and see how close I came."

Such statements not only build toward the result, but tend to draw keen minds from any suspicion of the simple but subtle secret on which this excellent trick depends.

Lucky Number Seven

This comes under the head of a mental mystery because the performer somehow always manages to divine the result. Such foresight can prove valuable, for if the performer wants to make this mystery a real thriller, he can stake some actual cash upon the outcome. In that case, careful rehearsal is advisable, rather than have foresight fail through oversight!

THE EFFECT

Seven pay envelopes are shown to the audience. These are small envelopes with flaps that open at the ends; any envelopes of this general pattern may be used.

In each of these envelopes, the performer places a folded slip of blank paper—with one exception. In the odd envelope he puts a folded dollar bill, so this promptly becomes the lucky envelope.

Now the problem is to find the lucky person. Stacking the envelopes, the magician states that he will deal them in rotation, leaving the outcome entirely to chance; hence, between each deal, he will systematically transfer envelopes from the top of the stack to the bottom. He illustrates this by moving an envelope from top to bottom, then dealing one, and moving another from top to bottom.

Here the performer pauses, hands the envelopes to a spectator and lets that person mix them in sideways shuffle fashion. Taking back the envelopes, the magician spreads them slightly, showing that there are just seven. Squaring the little packet, he goes through the dealing process, moving envelopes from top to bottom in between, until he has served six customers in regular fashion.

One envelope is left over, so the performer keeps it while the spectators eagerly open their envelopes to learn who was the lucky person. Indeed they will be very eager if the performer has specified that whoever has the dollar can keep it. By now the reader may have guessed who has the dollar in his envelope. That guess is right: the performer.

Always the magician winds up with the lucky envelope, leaving everyone else with blanks; six of them!

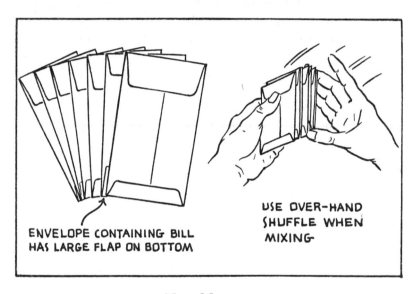

ENVELOPE CONTAINING BILL
HAS LARGE FLAP ON BOTTOM

USE OVER-HAND
SHUFFLE WHEN
MIXING

The Method

The whole trick depends upon the counting process; that is, the mode of transferring envelopes from top to bottom of the stack in connection with the deal. There are seven different systems, all natural and in keeping with the performer's preliminary statement. These systems apply according to the position of the "key" envelope, namely, the one that contains the dollar bill.

Therefore, before beginning the count out, the performer

must know the position of the key envelope. This is discovered by a simple but neat device. In first showing the envelopes, the performer has them arranged with all the flaps in one direction. In each he places a blank paper and seals the envelopes, still leaving the flaps pointing the same way, until he comes to the dollar envelope. He turns this envelope around after sealing it.

Thus when the envelopes have been shuffled sidewise fashion, the mere act of spreading them slightly enables the magician to note the position of the key envelope with its wrongly pointed end. He mentally counts its position from the top of the stack and proceeds with the particular counting deal that leaves him with the all-important envelope.

The dealing systems are as follows:

If the key envelope is on top of the stack, that is, at number one position, the performer designates six people as "first," "second," "third" and so on.

He then proceeds to transfer envelopes from the top of the stack to the bottom, spelling "F-I-R-S-T" and transferring an envelope for each letter until he reaches the final "T." On that letter, he deals an envelope to the first person. Then he transfers envelopes spelling "S-E-C-O-N-D," making the deal on the final letter "D." He continues with "T-H-I-R-D, F-O-U-R-T-H, F-I-F-T-H, S-I-X-T-H," always dealing on the last letter.

This leaves the performer with the seventh envelope, and it will be the money holder.

If the key envelope is second from the top of the stack, the performer numbers his victims from one to six. In transferring the envelopes he spells those numbers: "O-N-E" and deals an envelope on the letter "E." Similarly he spells "T-W-O," dealing an envelope on "O." He continues this up to six and keeps the seventh envelope for himself. The dollar will be in it.

When the key envelope is third from the top of the stack,

the performer says he hopes everybody will be lucky. So, in transferring the envelopes, he spells "L-U-C-K-Y," moving an envelope from top to bottom for *every letter*, because in this instance the performer must deal the *next* envelope after he completes the spelling transfer.

The performer will turn out to be the lucky person who has the dollar in his seventh envelope.

When the key envelope is fourth from the top of the stack, the performer deals the top card to the first spectator, saying "one." He then moves a card from top to bottom, saying "one," and deals the next card to the second spectator, saying "two." For the third spectator, he transfers two cards, counting "one, two," and deals the next card on the count of "three." He follows this process up to six, with one additional count for each number.

This leaves the magician with the money envelope as the seventh.

If the key envelope is at position five (from the top), use the "F-I-R-S-T, S-E-C-O-N-D" spelling system, right through to "S-I-X-T-H," but in this instance transfer an envelope from top to bottom for every letter so spelled, making the deal on the *next* card after each spelling is completed.

With the key envelope number six from the top there is no need to number the spectators at all. Simply deal an envelope to a spectator and put the next envelope under. Deal another and put the next under. Continue this until six persons have envelopes. Open the seventh and show the dollar.

When the key envelope is at number seven, the bottom of the stack, the system is to put the top envelope under, then deal the next. Again one under, then deal. Continue this straight through, keeping the seventh undealt envelope. It will contain the dollar.

PRESENTATION

Most points of presentation have been covered by the previous headings, but a few points should be emphasized. In stating that he will "count and deal" the performer merely indicates the process beforehand. Hence when he does the actual distribution his particular form of counting or spelling will be accepted as usual or uniform.

In telling someone to shuffle the envelopes, the performer should make a few sideways slides himself, indicating how it is to be done. This type of shuffle will keep the envelopes pointed in the proper directions. Not only should the performer watch to see that nothing goes wrong; after finishing his counting system he can check the final envelope to make sure it is pointed opposite to the rest.

The trick may be practiced with unsealed envelopes. In actual performance the performer can have a few extra envelopes handy with a key-chart (as illustrated) written or pasted on one. After spotting the position of the key envelope, the performer can pause to lay the extras aside and thus check the chart for the particular spelling system required.

A State of Mind

Seemingly a matter of mental coincidence, this experiment not only stands repetition, but seems to prove itself something more than mere chance when the same surprising result happens again and again. It's a neat trick, with its principle well disguised, and it works almost automatically.

THE EFFECT

The objects used are fifty-one small cards or slips of paper on which are typed the names of the United States and Puerto Rico. Along with these is a map depicting the states and the territory.

Dealing out ten cards each to as many as three persons, the performer tells each spectator to shuffle or mix his batch, draw one at random, and toss the rest back among the leftovers. Then the mental test begins.

The first person holds his card and spells the name of its state mentally, saying "go" as he thinks of each letter. The performer, studying the map, taps a state with his pencil, moving to another state each time the word "go" is repeated.

When the spectator has finished spelling the name he says "stay," which signifies that the performer is to keep the pencil exactly where it is. Then the person names the state aloud; the others look at the map.

The performer's pencil will be placed exactly on the state that the spectator has in mind!

The test may then be repeated with two other spectators, each of whom has selected a random card, and twice more the word "stay" will find the performer's pencil on the chosen state.

The Method

The names of the states and Puerto Rico offer a large variance in the number of letters found in their names. Running from four to thirteen letters each, there are at least three in every such group. This makes it possible to prepare three different lists of ten each, no two names on any one list having the same number of letters.

After preparing such lists, the performer arranges three groups of cards to correspond to them. He puts these groups in order on top of the little cards or slips that he has fixed for the trick. These cards are not in any rotation, like the lists. It is only necessary to have each group of ten cards together.

Thus the performer can first run through the cards, showing their names, and no one will suspect their secret. Turning them over, the performer counts off ten for each spectator, lets each select a card and toss back the rest. He is then ready to begin.

The lists are lying handy behind a book or some other object on the table where the map is placed. In tapping states, the performer makes the first three taps at random, preferably on states not listed in the groups. But his fourth tap is on the four-letter state that heads list one; his next tap on the five-letter state and so on, right down the list until the person halts him.

Whatever the chosen state, the performer will have struck it, apparently by mental coincidence but actually by simple numerical sequence. The same will apply to the names in list two and list three, when the performer concentrates on the other spectators.

Presentation

About the only point to stress in presentation is the fact that the cards contain the names of all the states and Puerto

Rico; hence the performer should run through them slowly and openly. No mention should be made of the fact that exactly ten cards are given to each person. Simply term each group "a batch" or "about a dozen cards."

The original packet may be arranged with a card from group one on top, then a card from group two, next a card from group three, and so on. In this case, the performer deals cards singly into three hands or groups for each spectator, deciding that he has dealt enough when he reaches ten.

Any sizable map will do. If Alaska, Hawaii and Puerto Rico are not on it, they should be marked in the upper left corner, the center left margin and lower right corner respectively.

Any of the unlisted states may be substituted to form a different list if the performer so desires, provided it is changed for a name of the same number of letters.

LIST ONE	LIST TWO	LIST THREE
OHIO	UTAH	IOWA
TEXAS	IDAHO	MAINE
OREGON	NEVADA	KANSAS
VERMONT	MONTANA	ARIZONA
MARYLAND	VIRGINIA	COLORADO
MINNESOTA	LOUISIANA	WISCONSIN
WASHINGTON	CALIFORNIA	PUERTO RICO
MISSISSIPPI	CONNECTICUT	RHODE ISLAND
WEST VIRGINIA	NEW HAMPSHIRE	PENNSYLVANIA
SOUTH CAROLINA	NORTH CAROLINA	MASSACHUSETTS

Here is an alphabetical list of the fifty states, plus Puerto Rico, from which the cards may be made up:

ALABAMA	INDIANA	NEBRASKA	RHODE ISLAND
ALASKA	IOWA	NEVADA	SOUTH CAROLINA
ARIZONA	KANSAS	NEW HAMPSHIRE	SOUTH DAKOTA
ARKANSAS	KENTUCKY	NEW JERSEY	TENNESSEE
CALIFORNIA	LOUISIANA	NEW MEXICO	TEXAS
COLORADO	MAINE	NEW YORK	UTAH
CONNECTICUT	MARYLAND	NORTH CAROLINA	VERMONT
DELAWARE	MASSACHUSETTS	NORTH DAKOTA	VIRGINIA
FLORIDA	MICHIGAN	OHIO	WASHINGTON
GEORGIA	MINNESOTA	OKLAHOMA	WEST VIRGINIA
HAWAII	MISSISSIPPI	OREGON	WISCONSIN
IDAHO	MISSOURI	PENNSYLVANIA	WYOMING
ILLINOIS	MONTANA	PUERTO RICO	

Spaces are not counted. Taps are made only on letters.

Unlisted Names. Numbers indicate total letters.

6—Alaska, Hawaii. 7—Wyoming, Indiana, Alabama, Georgia, New York, Florida. 8—Nebraska, Oklahoma, Missouri, Arkansas, Illinois, Michigan, Kentucky, Delaware. 9—New Mexico, Tennessee, New Jersey. 11—North Dakota, South Dakota.

Suit Yourself

Audience participation features this mental effect in which playing cards are used purely because of their adaptability to the experiment. Its principle subtly concealed, this mystery will bear a reasonable amount of repetition without losing its perplexity.

THE EFFECT

Several persons are each given four playing cards, all such cards being spot cards, as the performer is planning a mental experiment involving their values. Each person selects one of his cards, either looking at its face or making a blind choice, as he prefers, and all such cards—one from each cluster—are given an extra person, who looks at them exactly as if playing a hand in a card game.

The magician asks this person to name the number of clubs, diamonds, hearts or spades that he holds, these questions applying to *suits only*. At no time is anything asked regarding the *values* of the cards in the master hand. Yet from this the performer immediately names the total value of the cards in that random group. When their spots are added, the total proves exactly correct!

THE METHOD

To be effective, the trick should be performed with four, five or six groups of cards for the larger the number of groups, the more impressive the result. Each group contains a card of each suit, as follows:

First: two of clubs, three of diamonds, four of hearts, five of spades.

Second: three of clubs, four of diamonds, five of hearts, six of spades.

Third: four of clubs, five of diamonds, six of hearts, seven of spades.

Fourth: five of clubs, six of diamonds, seven of hearts, eight of spades.

Fifth: six of clubs, seven of diamonds, eight of hearts, nine of spades.

Sixth: seven of clubs, eight of diamonds, nine of hearts, ten of spades.

Each of these groups can be mixed independently; that is, its four cards do not have to be in any order of suits, but are merely handed to one person. Nor does the performer have to remember which person holds each group; he simply specifies that one card is to be drawn from each.

Assuming that all six groups are being used, the performer keeps in mind a *key number,* in this case 27. If it so happens that all six cards taken from the individual groups are *clubs,* this will represent the final total. So when the performer says to the man who holds the master hand: "How many clubs?" the answer can be ignored entirely.

But for every *diamond* the performer adds *one* to that total of 27. For every *heart* he adds *two.* For every *spade* he adds *three.* No matter what groups they come from, those extra numbers run true to form, giving the performer the precise total of 27 plus.

For example: suppose the master hand consists of the three of diamonds, three of clubs, six of hearts, seven of hearts, nine of spades, and eight of diamonds.

Told that there is one club, the performer ignores it and keeps his 27 in mind. When two diamonds are stated he adds *two* (one for each diamond) and brings his count to 29. Two hearts are announced so the performer adds *four* (two for each heart) making 33. One spade declared calls for an addition of *three* which makes the final total 36.

Working with only four people, the performer uses the first four groups and in this case his key number will be 14. For five people, the first five groups are used and the key number therefore is 20.

PRESENTATION

No mention should be made of the fact that the various groups contain one card of each suit, nor that there is any progression in their values. The magician simply states that he will give each spectator some cards, *all different* in value, so the person will have a choice of any number.

If the groups are set beforehand, the performer can draw them from the pack in individual clusters, giving each a face-up mix, then handing it to a person face down. However, he can use any borrowed pack and simply weed out batches of cards, his reason for picking them here and there being that he wants to make sure of having all different values in each group—at least that is his story.

It is good policy to suggest that each spectator choose a card at random by mixing his group face down and dealing one. Since each choice is individual, no person sees another's group, except at first glance; hence there is no chance of values being compared.

Unless the trick is to be repeated, all persons are told to toss their extra cards into a common discard; even if the trick is repeated, this should be done with its last showing. Mixing this discarded group when he picks it up, the performer disposes of all evidence that would suggest any arrangement.

In performing the trick for four persons, the magician may prefer to use the four highest groups with a key number of 22. Or for five people he can use the five highest groups with a key number of 26. All this is optional; in fact a multitude of variants are possible, according to how mathematically inclined the performer may be.

However, as given here, the rule is to have the cards in each group progress one unit, suit by suit, from clubs up through diamonds, hearts and spades. The determining factor in each instance will be the total value of the clubs, which constitutes the key number.

In performance it will be found that the total of each suit is known before spades are even mentioned. Therefore the spokesman can be stopped after naming the number of hearts, the performer simply adding three for each spade that he knows must be there. For example: one club, two diamonds, two hearts declared, means that there must be one spade to account for all members in a group of six people.

Mental Telegraphy

Originally, telepathy—or the transfer of messages from mind to mind—was styled "mental telegraphy." That title is peculiarly appropriate to the following mental effect, since it not only simulates thought reading, but involves an actual telegram in the course of its procedure.

THE EFFECT

Showing a sealed telegram, the magician places it in his inside pocket saying that it is a night message that he received but has not opened. Since such telegrams contain twenty-five words, the magician has prepared some paper slips bearing numbers from one to twenty-five inclusive, in order to undertake a mental test.

The slips are shown with their various numbers; folded, they are tossed into a hat and shaken. From the hat the magician removes three of the slips, tosses them on the table and asks the spectators which slip they would prefer to use. As they decide this, the performer hands the sealed telegram to another spectator.

Moving away or turning his back, the mental wizard requests that the chosen slip be unfolded and the telegram be opened. People are then to pick the word—in the telegram —that appears at the number on the slip. They are to concentrate upon that word, while the magician writes something on a large pad.

This done, the magician hands his result to the concentrating group and they find to their real surprise that he has named the very word on which their minds were focussed. A study of the telegram shows that it contains no two words alike, which further lessens the chance factor.

Of course it might all be a trick. Somehow the magician might have wangled three special slips into the game, all bearing the same number. But the two remaining slips are lying on the table and when opened their numbers prove different from that of the selected slip. The same applies to the slips that are still in the hat. They all contain different numbers, as the magician specified.

THE METHOD

First, it is necessary to compose *three* telegrams containing a number of identical words differently placed. The three given here are excellent, as they are all composed of the same twenty-five words; moreover, they are suited to the general theme of the mental mystery.

These telegrams look best when typed on regular telegraph blanks and sealed in the usual yellow envelopes; however, they can be improvised on ordinary paper. The audience is not aware that there are three telegrams. The performer keeps them in his inside pocket, arranged in order: "A," "B," and "C," these letters each referring to a telegram.

Before presenting the mystery, the performer selects a word that he intends to use. Let us suppose that the word is USE-LESS. It will be observed that this word appears at numbers 21, 19, and 6 in telegrams A, B, and C respectively. Therefore the performer must remove the slips that bear those numbers from the batch of twenty-five that are to be dropped in the hat. Incidentally, in preparing the slips, such numbers as 6 and 9 should be underlined so there will be no mistaking them.

The hat that the performer uses is of the felt or soft variety, with a divided crown. In one of these divisions the performer places the three slips (with numbers 21, 19, 6), taking care to place them in a line so that they can be removed in order later. For convenience, these slips will be termed "A," "B," and "C" to conform to the telegrams in the performer's pocket.

When the other slips—twenty-two in all—are dropped in the hat, the performer grips the hat from beneath, squeezing

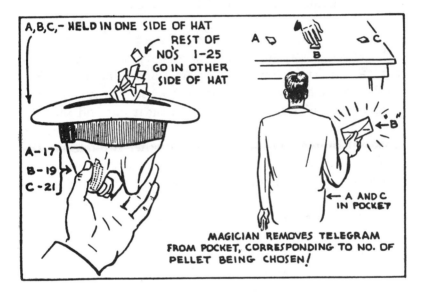

A,B,C,— HELD IN ONE SIDE OF HAT

REST OF NO'S 1-25 GO IN OTHER SIDE OF HAT

A   C

B

A-17
B-19
C-21

B"

A AND C IN POCKET

MAGICIAN REMOVES TELEGRAM FROM POCKET, CORRESPONDING TO NO. OF PELLET BEING CHOSEN!

the section or division which contains the three "forcing" slips. He may then shake the hat to mix the loose slips. Reaching into the hat, he takes out three slips one at a time, laying them in a row on the table. Apparently these have been drawn at random from the mixed slips. Actually, the performer relaxes his grip on the other half of the hat and takes out slips "A," "B," and "C" in order.

Asking the spectators to pick one of those slips, the performer reaches in his pocket for the telegram, delaying this just long enough to note which slip is taken. For slip A, he takes out telegram A; slip B calls for telegram B; slip C means to bring out telegram C.

Someone opens the slip and notes its number. The telegram is opened and the word at that number is the one on which people concentrate. Although the choice seems entirely ungoverned, the word—in this case USELESS—is predetermined. The performer writes that word on a pad as though he gained it as a mental impression.

PRESENTATION

An effective way to begin this mystery is by mentioning that it concerns a sealed telegram containing twenty-five words. Here the performer may simply state that he has the telegram in his pocket or he may bring it out and show it. In the latter case, he returns it to his pocket, making sure to replace it in its proper relation to the other two telegrams— a pair which the audience knows nothing about.

Replacing the telegram in the pocket is natural because the performer must have his hands free to show the slips. He states that there are twenty-five of these, but picks them up in a batch so that no one can count the exact number. He opens two or three of the slips, shows their numbers, then folds them and drops the lot into the hat.

If people want to see more of the slips and their numbers, the performer should remark that they can have that privilege later. In fact, if he can hold suspicion on the batch of slips, it is rather advisable to do so, since there is nothing whatever wrong with them, except that three are at present absent, which is the only fact to cover.

In bringing the three planted slips from the other section of the hat, the magician must of course remember their order. If this proves at all a problem, it can be easily rectified thus: In folding slip A, slant its second fold downward from its crease. Fold slip B straight along its crease. Slant the second fold of slip C upward from its crease.

Three slips thus folded can be handled carelessly and even mixed about, yet identified as soon as they are placed apart. Of course the original slips—the batch of twenty-two—should also be folded somewhat irregularly to conform to this situation.

Of course the performer can use various other words than USELESS. In fact, it is a good plan to change the word each time the trick is worked. For IMPOSSIBLE, the forcing slips would be as follows: A—11; B—3; C—25. For HAVE: A—8; B—12; C—20. For FOUND: A—9; B—1; C—5.

Instead of putting the slips in his hat, the performer can place them in his trousers pocket after first turning it inside out. In this case the three to be forced are tucked up in the corner of the pocket beforehand; they will remain hidden there when the pocket is apparently shown empty.

Of course those are the three slips that the performer later draws, either in rotation or in a bunch, but in the latter case they should be folded differently so that they be identified as A, B, or C in order to draw the corresponding telegram. At the finish, the bulk of the slips are brought from the pocket which is again turned inside out.

In summary, certain phases of the presentation come as a sequel to the mystery itself, such as going through the telegram to note that its words all differ; also, the opening of slips to prove that none bore the same number. Particular emphasis should be laid on the fact that the two slips on the table are different from the one finally taken. The performer can introduce this point by asking someone to open those slips to see what other words might have been chosen.

In all, this is one of the most subtle mental mysteries devised, because its real secret, the forcing of a word, seems an impossible explanation, inasmuch as the spectators have an absolutely free choice of three different slips that are taken from the hat. The artful and unsuspected device of the three telegrams—two of them unknown—is responsible for this result.

TELEGRAM "A"

SORRY THIS MESSAGE CONTAINS NOTHING IMPORTANT BUT HAVE FOUND IT IMPOSSIBLE TO GIVE DETAILS AND THEREFORE DECIDED TRYING WOULD BE USELESS IN SO FEW WORDS.

TELEGRAM "B"

FOUND IT IMPOSSIBLE IN SO FEW WORDS TO GIVE DETAILS AND HAVE THEREFORE DECIDED TRYING WOULD BE BUT USELESS   SORRY THIS MESSAGE CONTAINS NOTHING IMPORTANT.

TELEGRAM "C"

TRYING TO GIVE DETAILS FOUND USELESS IN SO FEW WORDS AND THEREFORE THIS MESSAGE CONTAINS NOTHING IMPORTANT   SORRY BUT HAVE DECIDED IT WOULD BE IMPOSSIBLE.

Color Sense

Tricks that stand repetition are comparatively uncommon and since this one fulfills that qualification it will prove very useful with the spectator whose constant plea is "Do it again." Indeed, this particular perplexity is one which should be done again—and again—in order to be thoroughly effective, because repeating it eliminates luck or guesswork.

The items used are simple and therefore easily prepared; merely three small squares of cardboard, cut to about the same size. Each of these squares is marked on both sides with colored crayon, preferably in a circle to emphasize the color, and every color is different. Thus there are six colors in all, which for convenience we shall list as red, orange, yellow, green, blue, and black.

The Effect

Using three small squares of cardboard, the performer turns them over to show that they bear different colors. He hands these to a spectator and asks him to place them on the table, with any colors up that he may choose.

From then on, the spectator is to turn over the squares, one at a time, as often as he wishes. He is to do this while the performer's back is turned, so there will be no way of guessing which particular square has been inverted. To make it even more confusing for the magician, the spectator may turn over any square as often as he wants; that is, he does not have to turn them in rotation. He has the privilege of turning any square repeatedly, or ignoring one altogether.

All the person must do is say "turn" every time he does so, thus enabling the magician to "sense" the color in question, although his back is turned. At the finish, the spectator places his hand over one of the squares, leaving the other two in view. Turning about, the performer then names the color that is showing in the upper side of the square beneath the spectator's hand.

From this description it is quite obvious that the magician would have an even chance of guessing the hidden color that

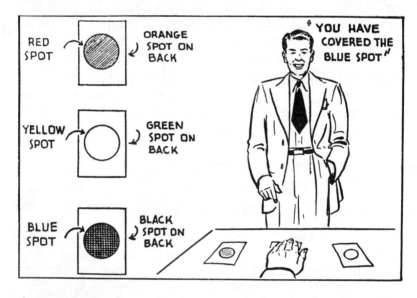

is uppermost beneath the person's hand. In turn, that proves why repetition makes this trick effective. By naming a hidden color time after time, the performer proves that something more than guesswork is involved and the more it is repeated, the more puzzled the witnesses become.

THE METHOD

The trick depends first of all upon the magician knowing the two colors on each square and also defining one side of each square as the "top" and the other as the "bottom." A simple system is to use the colors red, yellow and blue as "tops" and the intervening colors in spectrum order—orange, green, black—as "bottoms." The three squares will therefore be colored as follows:

First square: top—red, bottom—orange.
Second square: top—yellow, bottom—green.
Third square: top—blue, bottom—black.

Now to each of the top colors the performer gives a numerical value of one, while the bottom colors are zero. After the spectator has placed the three squares on the table and is ready to begin the turn-overs, the performer, by a mere glance, can add the total of the colors showing. If he sees only one of the three "top" colors, red, yellow or blue, he counts "one" to himself. If he sees two of those colors, he counts "two." Should all be showing, he mentally counts "three."

Once the performer's back is to the spectator and the latter begins to turn over the squares, the performer adds one point each time the spectator announces "turn." When the count ends, the performer can be certain of the result to this extent: If it finishes with an *odd* total, there will be an *odd* number of "tops" on the upper sides of the squares. If it finishes with an *even* total, there will be an *even* number of "tops" on display—or none.

From this information, the performer can easily divine the color showing on top of the square beneath the spectator's hand. A few examples will make this quite clear:

Spectator begins with red, green and blue. Two of those colors—red and blue—are "tops" so the performer mentally counts *two*. Spectator makes five turns, announcing them, and performer counts from two up to a total of seven. Spectator covers one square with his hand; the two the performer sees on view are yellow and blue. *Seven is odd,* so the "tops" must be *odd.* Therefore the hidden color is *red,* since only two "tops" are showing and there must be three in all.

Suppose the spectator begins with orange, yellow and black. There is only one "top," the yellow, so the performer starts his count from one. Suppose there are seven turns; the count arrives on *eight.* We then find the spectator covering one square, while the colors on the two that show are orange and green. *Eight* is *even,* so the "tops" can *not* be odd; that is, they must be an even number (two) or zero. Since the two colors showing (orange and green) are "bottoms," the hidden color must be a "bottom" also. Therefore the magician announces it to be *black.*

Note: The examples given simply illustrate the rule, not the exact result. For instance: beginning with red, blue and green, and making five turns, you might end with yellow and black showing. The *seven* total being *odd,* you must have an odd number of "tops." Therefore since one "top" —yellow—is showing, and one "bottom"—black—the hidden color must be a "bottom" which in this case is green.

In brief, you divine the hidden color by a process of logic or elimination.This becomes very simple after you have practiced it and familiarized yourself with the system. To practice the trick, place the squares on the table, note their colors, and look away while you turn over the squares at random, counting the number of turns. Then place your hand over one square and take a look at the other two. Name the hidden color and raise your hand to see if you are right.

Of course a brief amount of "concentration" is allowable, in fact effective, before naming the hidden color; so your practice should be considered in terms of accuracy, not speed.

FAMOUS STAGE
ILLUSIONS

FAMOUS STAGE
ILLUSIONS

THE most spectacular development in the art of modern magic was that of the stage illusion, which rose to prominence at the turn of the century and has since then held a place of permanent importance. The stage illusion, so-called, can be generally defined as a magical effect involving either human beings or bulky objects that are too sizable to be manipulated by the aid of sleight-of-hand or apparatus that the performer can manage individually.

Choice of the term "illusion" to describe such effects is quite appropriate, because whatever the device employed, even though strictly mechanical, it is quite obvious that something more than mere personal skill is required to accomplish the desired deception. Therefore the result is an illusion from the observer's standpoint, even though factors other than optics or acoustics are brought to bear.

As for the fuller definition of "stage illusion," it covers the fact that most of these ambitious magical effects were designed to meet the requirements of the theater, where magic, like other forms of dramatic art, was regarded better as it grew bigger. This placed exacting conditions upon magicians, since they were forced to make their creations stupendous, yet at the same time gave them certain advantages found only on the stage.

It is true that in aiming for the sensational the stage illusion became overdeveloped and restricted to use in its particular field. This however applied chiefly to vaudeville, where acts were presented under high-pressure and novelty was ever the vogue. The legitimate magic show, a full evening's entertainment in itself, maintained its place despite the changes in the magical scene and, as a result, the names of Herrmann, Kellar, Thurston, and Blackstone form an unbroken line of great illusionists over a period of more than half a century.

There were many others who specialized in big magic, though sometimes only briefly, and the net result was an amazing application of ingenuity and mechanics to the singular task of entertaining the public by amazing it. Of the devices thus employed, certain of the most intriguing have been selected for explanation in this book.

Rather than utilize space in describing the various subdivisions of stage illusions from the standpoints of effect and method, this section will be devoted to the description of individual illusions themselves, each covering some distinct phase of an art belonging to the men who were truly the masters of modern magic.

Here we shall find impossibilities made real, with the secrets revealed in sufficient detail not only to satisfy those readers with a thirst for magical knowledge, but to inspire others who may cherish the ambition to become the great stage magicians of the future.

Sawing a Woman in Half

Evolved from a "decapitation trick" performed four centuries ago, the illusion of "sawing a woman in half" was developed from a comedy stunt presented about 1890, wherein a clown was placed beneath a sheet on an eight-legged couch which was then sawed in half, clown and all.

Some thirty years later, several vaudeville magicians suddenly shocked their jaded and sophisticated audiences by introducing baffling versions of the "sawing" as the theatrical sensation of the early Twenties. Principal among these performers were Selbit, Goldin, and Leon, who seem to have produced their respective versions of the illusion in the order named.

Most sensational of all the presentations was the Goldin version, which so captured public interest that a whole group of magicians was required to take out additional units and thus meet the immediate demand. The Goldin version was also acquired by Thurston who presented it as a regular feature with his full evening show.

As a result, the Goldin version rapidly eclipsed all others and since it was the most baffling as well as the most spectacular illusion of its day, it is the version described herewith.

THE EFFECT

On the stage stands an isolated platform upon which is a box about five feet long and three feet wide, its broad side fronting toward the audience. The box is divided into two sections, with doors in front, top and back.

After inviting a committee on the stage, the magician hypnotizes a girl, whose rigid body is lifted by two straps attached to ropes and lowered into the box, where the girl's head emerges at one end, her feet at the other. The ends of the box are fitted with stocks, or pillories, one pair encasing

the girl's ankles, the other pair accommodating her neck and wrists.

The girl's hands and feet are held by two members of the committee; the doors are then closed and the magician proceeds to saw the box in half, using a huge cross-cut saw maneuvered by himself and an assistant. When the saw reaches the platform it is removed and two square slabs are inserted down between the divided sections. The halves of the box are then slid apart, the girl's head and hands still projecting from one end, her feet from the other.

Afterward the box is pushed together, the slabs removed, the stocks unlocked, and the doors are opened so that the girl can be lifted out. Awakened from her trance, she proves to be quite intact and utterly unharmed by the saw; hence the audience is more stupefied than ever.

The Method

Two girls are used in the illusion. The extra girl is concealed in the platform beneath the long box. After the doors are closed, the original girl draws her feet from their half of the box and doubles herself in the other half. The extra girl pushes her knees up through a trap in the platform and extends her feet through that end of the box.

This all happens after the doors of the box are closed, hence the spectators fancy that they still see the head and feet of one girl. After the box is sawed in half, the slabs are pushed down between so that the spectators can not see into the sections when they are separated. The top half of the box is slid away from the lower half because the extra girl is in a fixed position within the platform and therefore can not be moved.

Restoring the divided lady is simply a reversal of the process. The halves of the box are pushed together, the slabs are removed, the extra girl draws her feet down into the platform and the original girl stretches full length in the box.

PRESENTATION

Much could be written on the presentation of this fine illusion, which actually constituted an entire magic act in itself. The most essential feature, in fact one on which the whole success of the mystery depends, is the switch or exchange of feet, as worked by the original girl and the extra.

To convince the audience that all is fair, the magician actually locks the first girl's ankles in the lower pair of stocks, before the doors of the box are closed. This is a real convincer and, to nullify it, the magician adds what seems at the time to be another convincing factor.

To prove that the girl is really locked, the performer and his assistants turn the platform on wheels so that the head end is toward the audience. A committee man is already holding the girl's hands and the magician shows that the stocks are securely locked.

The lower end of the box is then *away* from the audience. Not only are its stocks neatly faked so that the lower half can hinge inward, allowing the girls to make the switch of feet; the man holding the girl's ankles is actually a confederate from the audience, who allows this to take place. The box is then swung clear around so that the magician can show that the girl's ankles are held while he rattles the solid locks on the frame of the tricked stocks.

After the restoration of the girl, a similar procedure takes place. The head end of the box is turned toward the audience so that the stocks can be unlocked; meanwhile the switch of feet is happening at the other end, which is later turned toward the audience and unlocked.

The finest bit of stage business in the presentation of the sawing illusion is as follows: after the girl is presumably sawed in half, the magician commands her to move her hands and feet, which she does. The man who is holding the girl's feet promptly expresses doubt that they are real—an excellent touch, since he happens to be the magician's confederate! —so the magician removes one of the girl's shoes. Then, further to convince the "skeptic," the magician draws up the tip of the stocking and clips it off to reveal the girl's toes which are seen to be quite genuine.

The magician keeps the shoe; hence after the girl is hoisted from the box, the spectators see that she is wearing only one shoe and that her stocking has a clipped toe. But this is the original girl—the only one the audience knows about— whereas it was the extra girl whose shoe was removed and whose stocking was clipped!

The explanation is simply that the original girl wears a toeless stocking from the start and kicks off her corresponding shoe while in the box. The other girl reaches up through the trap and brings the odd shoe down into the platform. Simple enough to persons who know how the illusion works, but to the average onlooker this is another bit of "evidence" that keeps him thinking in terms of one girl only.

Such are the subtle points that are found in the proper presentation of an effective stage illusion.

Vanishing Girl and Piano

One of the most ambitious of stage illusions is that of the "vanishing piano," accompanied by the lady who is playing it. This effect was designed to meet the demand for larger and more spectacular mysteries and it incorporates certain subtle features that illustrate the psychological factors behind a large-scale deception.

THE EFFECT

On a wheeled platform near the side of the stage a young lady is seated at an upright piano. As she begins to play the piano, the magician's assistants wheel the platform around, whereupon the pianist interrupts her music by angrily striking a succession of discords.

Promptly the magician orders his assistants to lower the curtains of a square canopy which is hanging above the platform by a heavy rope. Once this is done, the girl begins to play a subdued melody, which comes muffled from within the curtains, but the magician is in no mood for music.

After the curtains have been hooked to the platform, the magician ends the piano concert with a series of pistol shots at the cabinet. Immediately the music stops; the canopy is hoisted and its curtains come falling to the platform, where they flatten.

Girl, bench and piano, all have vanished, leaving only the platform which proves absolutely bare after the assistants gather up the loose curtains and carry them away.

THE METHOD

The deception begins from the moment the girl starts to play the piano. Actually the music comes from a piano off

stage, because the piano at which the girl is seated is merely a dummy contrivance, hinged to pack in very small space. Since the platform is at that side of the stage, the music arrives from the proper direction, producing a perfect illusion.

As soon as the curtains are lowered over the platform, the girl lifts a hinged trap in the front third of the platform, folds special hinged legs up under the bench and stows the latter in a shallow compartment beneath the trap.

Similarly she lifts a trap in the center third of the platform, folds the front of the piano downward in two hinged sections with the dummy keyboard flattening likewise and closes the trap.

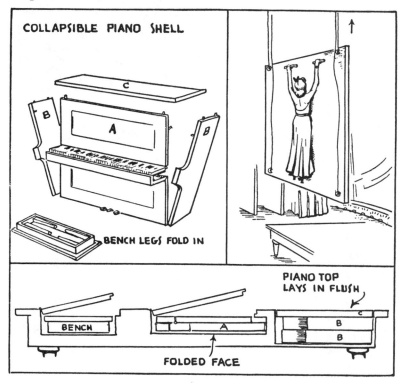

Meanwhile the magician's assistants are squaring the curtains around the platform. One man, standing behind the platform is actually folding the top of the piano down over the back, which doubles so that all three sections hinge into a hidden space or well, occupying the rear third of the platform. The inside of the piano top is painted to match the platform, hence the well, when filled, becomes level with the platform proper.

The girl then grips handles set beneath the solid frame-work that forms the canopy. These are arranged so that her weight is forward; hence the canopy tilts in that direction when it is hoisted. The curtains are dropped by an automatic release but, by the time they fall, the top of the canopy is squarely toward the audience, hiding the girl behind it.

PRESENTATION

As with every large illusion, proper timing, careful rehearsal, and good-working equipment are essential. The off-stage piano plays subdued notes, producing a muffled effect while the girl and the man behind the platform are packing away the dummy items. The girl gives a signal when ready and, with the magician's pistol shots, the real piano stops playing and the canopy is hoisted.

The audience, thinking in terms of the piano which they have accepted as an object of considerable bulk and weight, immediately discount the tilting canopy and concentrate upon the floundering curtains. As they realize that the piano could not be beneath that settling mass, they suspect that the girl at least might be.

By the time the curtains have been gathered and the platform shown bare, the canopy frame has gone out of sight above the scenery that borders the top of the stage. Most persons never realize that it tilted forward, nor that it was a solid square instead of an open framework.

The Invisible Flight

From the day it was first presented, this illusion became and remained one of the greatest sensations in the realm of stage magic. Much controversy followed regarding its origination, the chief disputants being two famous illusionists: Horace Goldin and Gustave Fasola.

Apparently both had a claim because after Goldin brought legal proceedings against Fasola in England, both continued to perform the illusion and it was later featured by Howard Thurston in America. Year after year it amazed and intrigued those who witnessed its performance, whether they had seen it before or for the first time.

Though as good today as ever, the "invisible flight" has faded from magical repertoires because it belongs with the full-stage type of show that is less prevalent than formerly, and also because it depends upon contrivances that are not commonly used. As a spectacular effect it still stands unique, as will be evident from its description.

THE EFFECT

A huge cannon is wheeled on the stage and a girl is loaded into its gaping mouth, sliding completely out of sight within the cannon. The big gun is turned and aimed at a box that is hanging from the dome of the theater. The cannon is fired with a loud report and a huge gush of flame and smoke issue from its muzzle.

The box, a cubical affair measuring some four feet in each direction is hauled down from the dome by a rope to which it is attached. Set on the stage, the box is opened and another box is taken from within it. This box too is opened and a third box lifted out.

Placed on a pedestal, the final box is unlocked and, when its lid is lifted, out pops the girl from a compact space barely large enough to contain her. Apparently she was fired invisibly from the cannon into the very center of the three nested boxes!

THE METHOD

Contrary to common belief, the girl from the nest of boxes is *not* a double packed therein before the show began. The small size of the box and its solidity are two factors which should dispel this theory; nevertheless it persisted, probably because there seemed no other possible explanation.

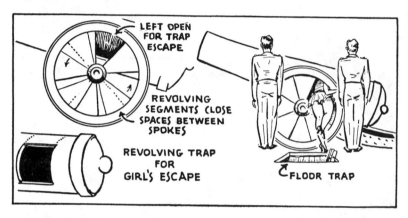

To cover the route that the girl really travels, it is necessary first to consider her disappearance from the cannon, which is by no means a trifling mystery in itself.

The cannon has two wheels. These are fitted with wide ornamental spokes, tapering outward from the axle, but with open segments in between. The cannon is sideways to the audience when the girl climbs a ladder and starts her slide down into the muzzle. At the rear of the cannon, on either side of the far wheel, are two assistants standing there as if to steady the contrivance, but actually their purpose is more subtle.

One of these assistants pulls a release attached to the rear wheel and a set of inner spokes revolve to close the gaps between the solid ones. This is not noticed by the audience because they are viewing the rear wheel through the cut-outs of the front one; hence their observation is limited.

When the gaps in the rear wheel are filled, the spectators are still deceived because they take it for granted that the rear wheel has openings and suppose that other persons are gaining a view clear through, from other angles. Each person thinks that mere chance has brought the rear spokes to a position that cuts off his own observation.

The assistants crowd close beside the wheel, because the girl comes through a faked section of the cannon that is located right between them. Meanwhile, a stage trap has opened in the space that the assistants flank. The girl goes right through, her drop behind the cannon wheel being covered from the sides by the presence of the assistants, one of whom brings back the false spokes the moment that the girl is through the stage and the trap has closed.

Thus the spectators, by the time they start to think about it, are actually gaining a clear view through the wheels of the cannon, which is promptly pivoted around to show it from all sides and is finally aimed toward the hanging box at the top of the theater.

Now for the girl's reappearance.

While the empty gun is being fired upward, the girl is being placed beneath a trap in the center of the stage. But she is not merely taking a position there; it would be impossible, even for a magician, to project a girl, doubled like a jackknife, up into a nest of boxes, particularly since the inner box must definitely be shown solid.

This produces a technical problem with a most ingenious solution.

The third or innermost box is not in the hanging nest at all. It is below stage, waiting for the girl when she does the drop behind the cannon. The girl is packed into the box, which is just large enough to contain her comfortably, and the box itself is set below the trap.

When the big box from the theater dome arrives on the stage it is set directly over the trap, as indicated by upright metal markers. A cue is given to the crew beneath the stage and, while the pulley and ropes are being detached from the big box, the little one with the girl included is shot up through the stage.

There are actually two boxes on the stage, one within the other, and both have flap bottoms that hinge upward to receive the genuine box that contains the girl. When the largest box is opened, another is drawn out, and with this intermediate box comes the all-important one, thanks to interior catches that hook it inside the second member of the nest.

The second box is brought forward, opened rapidly, and the innermost box is drawn up from within it. This is done quite rapidly and the final box is immediately brought further forward to the pedestal so that it is clear of the stage. There it is opened and the girl springs into view.

PRESENTATION

From the explanation of this illusion, it is obvious that much time must be spent upon its rehearsal, since so many persons, seen and unseen, participate in the execution. The magician, however, is chiefly concerned with two factors: one, to impress the audience with the fact that only one girl is involved; the other, to emphasize the isolation of the final box from which the girl reappears.

To cover the first point, a handkerchief is borrowed from the audience and tied around the girl's arm. Afterward, that same handkerchief is taken from her arm and returned to the owner, proof in itself that the girl could have traveled from the cannon into the box, since the handkerchief unquestionably did so.

As for the business in opening the boxes, there is an added device that allows extra time beyond the removal of the ropes and pulley. The middle box already being in the outer, the latter can be opened before the inner box arrives

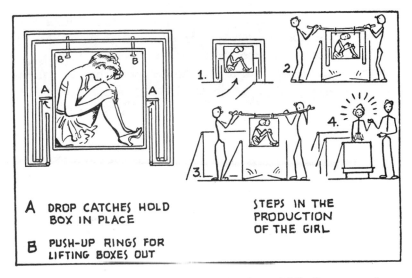

A   DROP CATCHES HOLD
     BOX IN PLACE

B   PUSH-UP RINGS FOR
     LIFTING BOXES OUT

STEPS IN THE
PRODUCTION
OF THE GIRL

through the trap.   In order to lift the middle box, two iron rings are inserted in it, and a pole is thrust through these. This takes time, hence the outer box can be opened fairly rapidly, letting the expectant audience see what is inside it.

If there is delay below stage, trouble is experienced in pushing the pole through the iron rings. Such trouble, however, only occurs when the second box is drawn out. The final box, the one containing the girl, also has a pair of metal loops to conform to the general arrangement. It is always lifted rapidly, with as little delay as possible, because by then the trick is as good as done, and there is never any waiting for a cue.

In illusions of this type, one action follows another so promptly that the average person seldom traces back to what occurred before. Thus the quick lifting of the third box causes everyone to forget any previous fumbling or delay. Likewise, the setting of the solid box upon the pedestal implies—when the trick is mentally reviewed—that the first and second boxes were similarly isolated.

Despite this psychological handling of the climax, the illusion must be smartly presented through every phase. Any blundering that seems unnatural will make a bad impression that may persist, no matter how smooth the subsequent action may be.

The Bangkok Bungalow

For sheer ingenuity and bold presentation, the "Bangkok bungalow" stands unequalled. It not only illustrates the psychology of deception at its best, but proves that there is an art in demonstrating large illusions which rivals the skill required in sleight-of-hand.

All the principles of misdirection apply with the "bungalow," but they are translated in terms of showmanship instead of dexterity. The result is a daring disappearance accomplished under the closest scrutiny, which makes the climax all the more bewildering.

Here is a case where people are told to "see and believe" but refuse to do so. By the time they have rejected the real explanation of the mystery, they are gulled along a false trail from which their minds are unable to return.

THE EFFECT

On the stage stands a large, heavily curtained cabinet with a thick canopy top. These are factors which immediately excite suspicion, especially when the performer ignores them and emphasizes instead that the cabinet floor is well above the level of the stage, so that no one could possibly enter or leave by that direction.

The curtains are slid open but, being heavy, they bunch and might therefore conceal someone at a rear corner of the cabinet. The magician ignores this also, because he is busy telling the audience about the Bangkok bungalow, a remarkable miniature house that he brought back from Siam.

The little bungalow is brought on stage and it is small indeed, measuring only a little more than two feet in each direction, including the slanted roof above its squarish walls. It is stoutly constructed, however, and of heavy wood, weighty enough so that an assistant helps the magician lift it up to the high floor of the curtained cabinet.

This bungalow, the magician avows, is the home of a Siamese dancing girl, who was reduced to doll dimensions by the same process of Oriental magic that compressed the bungalow from full house size. The magician speaks to the occupant and a tiny voice answers, but since the magician is partly turned away, the spectators recognize that he is dealing only in a bit of ventriloquism as a byplay to his story.

The bunched curtains are drawn along their rods, thus concealing the tiny house in the large cabinet. The magician calls for the girl to step from the bungalow, then waves

GIRL CONCEALED BY CURTAIN AT START

CURTAIN

CONSPICUOUS BULGE AFTER VANISH IS A HANGING RING THAT GIRL LEAVES HORIZONTALLY

WIRE TO FLIES TAKES THE WEIGHT TO GIVE THE ILLUSION OF LIGHTNESS AS ASS'T. CARRIES DOLL HOUSE OFF-STAGE HOUSE SWINGS WITH PENDULUM ACTION

his hands as a magic gesture that will cause her to gain her real size. The front curtain is opened, and there stands the dancing girl, beside the knee-high bungalow.

Quite puzzled by the fact that the audience is not amazed, the magician states that he will reduce the girl again and send her back into the bungalow. The curtain is drawn, the hand wave is reversed, and when the curtain is opened, the girl is gone.

To prove that the dancer has actually vanished, the magician has an assistant lift out the little house. The magician steps into the cabinet and whips open the rear curtain so that people can look right through. The assistant carries the tiny bungalow away and the mystery is complete—except for a few unfortunate details.

The canopy top and the side curtains still loom large, particularly the curtain on the left. It has a distinct bulge indicating that it is double, with the girl concealed between. Noting this, the magician strikes the curtain and the bulge leaves it. Then he begins snatching the curtains from their hooks, bundling them and tossing them to assistants. Finally, the magician whips down the canopy, bundles it into an empty mass and flings it to the stage.

There stands the magician alone in a cabinet which has been reduced to a thin floor with skeleton rods and uprights, lacking sufficient space to hide the vanished girl even if she had been magically reduced to the size of an average doll!

THE METHOD

The girl is actually hidden in a bunched corner curtain at the outset. It is the rear curtain and she stays behind it, entering the cabinet after the front has been closed. After the vanish, however, she does not go between the double curtain on the left. The bulge that the audience sees is a metal ring which the girl turns horizontally between the curtain folds, to make people think she is still there.

After that, the girl leaves the cabinet unseen. The question is, where does she go—and how? The answer is the very thing the magician tells the audience.

The girl goes away in the little house!

Simply a shell with no back, the house easily receives the

girl who is slender and supple. When the cabinet curtains are closed, the girl doubles herself into the tiny bungalow, which appears particularly diminutive in contrast to the large size of the cumbersome cabinet.

The added weight that the girl gives the bungalow is nullified by another factor that the audience does not suspect. Running down from the flies above the stage is a strong but thin piano wire with a hook attached. Before cramming into the bungalow, the girl takes the hook from a cabinet post where it is fixed and loops it into a metal ring concealed in the half-slant of the bungalow roof.

This wire is drawn taut from off stage so when the assistant picks up the little house, he is burdened by only a portion of its weight and thus can carry it off stage as though it were as light as when he brought it to the cabinet.

If the cabinet is fairly close to the wing, the carrying of the house can simply be a swing-off, the wire coming into the front of the cabinet at an angle from the wing. For a longer carry, the wire comes from directly above and is trolleyed along from a batten above the scenery at the same speed as the assistant's pace.

Thus the girl is really gone—and in the bungalow—before the magician begins to tear down the cabinet to convince the audience that he told them a truth that they still refuse to believe!

PRESENTATION

During the first stages of the illusion, the performer constantly encourages the audience to suspect the cabinet and therefore accept the bungalow purely as a somewhat inadequate device intended to draw their attention from those telltale curtains. The arrival of the girl within the cabinet increases this misplaced suspicion.

The crux comes when the bungalow is taken from the

cabinet. The bulge in the curtain on the left carries attention in that direction and, as the assistant starts his walk-off, the performer draws straying eyes back to the cabinet by stepping through and whipping away the rear curtain, which only makes the side bulge the more obvious.

Once the assistant is off stage, the magician banishes the bulge by knocking the ring flat between the double curtain. From then on, the action is rapid and convincing, curtains and canopy being bundled and flung with such abandon that the audience is left in total amazement when the performer steps down from the completely empty cabinet and takes his bow.

Walking Through a Brick Wall

Originally presented at St. George's Hall, a little theater in London that specialized exclusively in magical entertainment, the illusion of "walking through a wall" attracted the attention of Houdini, who promptly bought it outright.

Returning to America, Houdini therewith transplanted this mystery from one of the world's smallest theaters to the largest, booking it at the New York Hippodrome. Highly advertised, the illusion proved its worth as a box-office attraction, bringing more customers to the Hippodrome in a single week than St. George's Hall could have gathered in an entire season.

Commercially, "walking through a wall" unquestionably established a unique record, while from a magical standpoint it is in a category very much its own, due to unusual factors both in its method and its presentation.

THE EFFECT

Members of the audience are invited on the stage to inspect a large metal framework some eight feet high by twelve feet long and a foot or so in width. The base of this framework is mounted on small rollers so that it can be wheeled about.

The stage itself is covered by a large rug or carpet of plain pattern. This rug is inspected also, so the committee can make sure that there is no possibility of a trap door figuring in the approaching mystery. The frame is then wheeled to the exact center of the stage and turned endwise toward the audience.

Brick masons then take over. Using a supply of bricks and mortar provided for the purpose, they rapidly build a solid wall within the framework, which may be turned to show both surfaces of the completed wall, but is finally left in its endwise position, like a partition dividing the two sides of the stage.

Two screens are set against the opposite sides of the brick wall. Each screen forms three sides of a square, the wall itself being the fourth. The wall being taller than the screens, the top of the wall can be seen above them. The magician enters one screen and encloses himself in its square, while the spectators form an outspread cordon around the wall, watching every angle.

A short while later the screen on the other side of the wall opens and out steps the performer. The first screen is immediately removed from its side of the wall and that space is found vacant.   To all appearances the magician has somehow worked himself through a brick wall which remains as solid as ever!

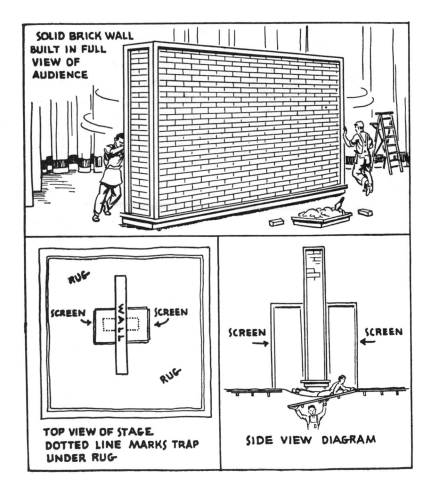

SOLID BRICK WALL BUILT IN FULL VIEW OF AUDIENCE

RUG

SCREEN   WALL   SCREEN

RUG

TOP VIEW OF STAGE
DOTTED LINE MARKS TRAP
UNDER RUG

SCREEN   SCREEN

SIDE VIEW DIAGRAM

The Method

Despite the fact that a stage trap is ruled out of the proceedings, its use is the actual explanation of this riddle. How a trap could be employed when covered with a rug is a problem in itself, yet not too puzzling when properly analyzed.

The performer does not have to drop through a trap to come up on the far side of the wall. All he needs is enough space to squeeze himself under the base of the frame. He gains this by means of a wide trap door that includes the spaces surrounded by the screens as well as the intervening wall.

As soon as the magician is within one screen, the trap is lowered. The rug sags as he worms his way under the wall. As soon as he reaches the other screen, the hidden trap is raised and again clamped in place from beneath the stage. The rug is a very large one, hence its draw toward the center is unnoticed when it takes the performer's weight. In relation to the large area of the rug, the sag is extremely slight, and when the trap is raised, the rug becomes reasonably smooth again.

Presentation

In its full presentation this illusion takes considerable time because of the building of the wall; hence it constitutes an act in itself. If performed as a feature of a regular show, the wall should be built in advance and inspected in that condition, cutting the running time to as few as ten minutes.

Otherwise, the presentation consists chiefly of letting the committee inspect everything in sight, both before and after the mystery is accomplished. Secret cues for the man beneath the stage complete the list of requirements.

The Vanishing Automobile

This illusion, presented by Thurston as the finale of his full-evening show, was probably the most highly advertised of any individual stage attraction ever exhibited by a magician. During the years that Thurston performed the illusion, huge lithographs were posted in every city he played, portraying the automobile in the course of its disappearance with a squad of passengers.

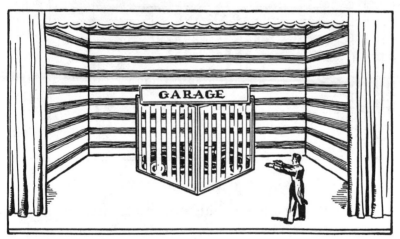

While planned largely for box-office appeal, the disappearance of the automobile occurred regularly as advertised, and in order to uphold its claims the illusion necessarily had to be a good one. There was another factor: In order to avoid cost of transporting the automobile as baggage, or hiring someone to drive it from city to city, cars of a nationally known make were supplied locally, as a publicity arrangement. This tie-up with the automobile dealers meant that they would have to be satisfied too.

Hence, considerable money was spent on the illusion, part of the cost involving rather elaborate experiment as will be evident from the detailed description of the automobile's evanishment. Nevertheless, the equipment was comparatively light and portable, considering the size of the object vanished.

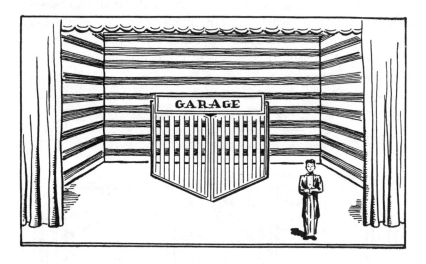

The Effect

On a full stage, boxed with striped curtains, at the rear stands a garage of open-work pattern. This structure has **two** walls formed of upright slats with spaces between them; the corner where the walls meet is pointing toward the audience.

Above, covering the right angle thus formed, is a slanted roof, bearing the word "GARAGE." An automobile of the roadster type, carrying several passengers, is rolled on stage and wheeled into the garage from the open back, so that the car and its occupants show plainly through the slatted openings of the angled walls.

Quite isolated on the stage, the automobile seems to have but one possible chance of exit, namely, down through the stage itself, which would doubtless be a slow and cumbersome

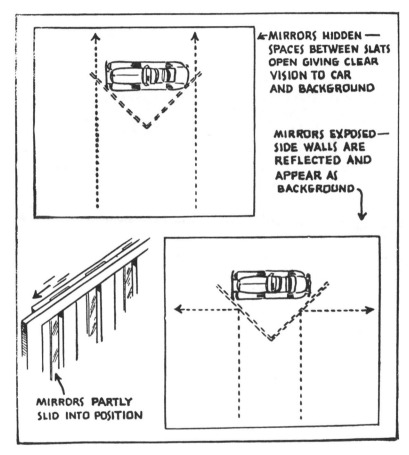

←MIRRORS HIDDEN — SPACES BETWEEN SLATS OPEN GIVING CLEAR VISION TO CAR AND BACKGROUND

MIRRORS EXPOSED— SIDE WALLS ARE REFLECTED AND APPEAR AS BACKGROUND

MIRRORS PARTLY SLID INTO POSITION

process, possible only if the car were hidden from view for at least a dozen seconds. That possibility is immediately nullified. The magician fires a pistol shot and the car vanishes instantly, leaving complete vacancy beyond the open walls that were never hidden from sight!

The Method

The "vanishing automobile" represents a somewhat elaborate development of a mirror principle used with magical illusions.   The stage is boxed, so that the side curtains with their horizontal stripes will correspond exactly with the rear curtain, particularly in their distance from the slatted walls of the garage.

By placing mirrors behind those slats, the vision of the spectators is deflected at an angle of forty-five degrees, so that the eye mistakes the reflection of the side curtains for the rear. This holds true when viewed from the sides of the auditorium as well as the front.   Any downward view from the second balcony is cut off by the comparatively small roof above the slatted walls.

Not single mirrors, but a succession of narrow ones, are used.   This is possible because the slats are slightly wider than the spaces between them.   The mirrors themselves are metal slats, set in a framework and they are hidden behind the wider pickets that form the walls of the garage.   The frames slide above and below the pickets; when actuated by a release, they spring over and draw the mirrors to fill the intervening openings in the garage walls.

Presentation

Except for the preliminary task of setting the stage so that the slatted mirrors will reflect perfectly when in place, the presentation of this illusion would seem quite simple, but such is not the case.   The noise of the sliding mirrors can be reduced or drowned by the orchestra, but the action itself is visible.

Three methods have been used to cover the brief but telltale flash of the mirrors as they flick to their position between the slats.   The first way is to extinguish the lights for a matter of a few seconds, bringing them on again so promptly that the automobile would not have time to be removed but is never-theless gone. This form of presentation is generally unsatisfactory, as it connotes trickery.

A highly effective presentation is with the use of flash powder, set off automatically with the release of the mirrors. The burst of light and its attendant smoke cover the movement of the mirrors; nevertheless such a presentation has one serious drawback. In an illusion of this size, a battery of flash pots is required and the flare either blinds the audience or fills the stage with too much smoke. Gauged to the proper balance it is excellent, but finding that point is difficult.

The third and perhaps most startling presentation is with the aid of a large spotlight and a blinker. The spot concentrates upon the garage and the portion of the stage surrounding it, showing the car and the people very plainly. The blinker is a disk with pie-shaped cutouts that is spun in front of the spotlight producing a rapid change of alternating light and darkness, an uncanny effect in itself.

This is the equivalent of the spectators blinking their own eyes while the mirrors slide in place and, though they do not lose sight of the garage, the peculiar blur covers the motion of the mirrors and causes a fadeout effect in which the automobile vanishes. When the stage lights come on and the blinker ends its sequence, people find themselves staring into the apparently empty garage, wondering how the automobile managed to dissolve itself, passengers and all.

A CATALOG OF SELECTED
DOVER BOOKS
IN ALL FIELDS OF INTEREST

A CATALOG OF SELECTED DOVER
BOOKS IN ALL FIELDS OF INTEREST

DRAWINGS OF REMBRANDT, edited by Seymour Slive. Updated Lippmann, Hofstede de Groot edition, with definitive scholarly apparatus. All portraits, biblical sketches, landscapes, nudes. Oriental figures, classical studies, together with selection of work by followers. 550 illustrations. Total of 630pp. 9⅛ × 12¼.
21485-0, 21486-9 Pa., Two-vol. set $29.90

GHOST AND HORROR STORIES OF AMBROSE BIERCE, Ambrose Bierce. 24 tales vividly imagined, strangely prophetic, and decades ahead of their time in technical skill: "The Damned Thing," "An Inhabitant of Carcosa," "The Eyes of the Panther," "Moxon's Master," and 20 more. 199pp. 5⅜ × 8½. 20767-6 Pa. $4.95

ETHICAL WRITINGS OF MAIMONIDES, Maimonides. Most significant ethical works of great medieval sage, newly translated for utmost precision, readability. Laws Concerning Character Traits, Eight Chapters, more. 192pp. 5⅜ × 8½.
24522-5 Pa. $4.50

THE EXPLORATION OF THE COLORADO RIVER AND ITS CANYONS, J. W. Powell. Full text of Powell's 1,000-mile expedition down the fabled Colorado in 1869. Superb account of terrain, geology, vegetation, Indians, famine, mutiny, treacherous rapids, mighty canyons, during exploration of last unknown part of continental U.S. 400pp. 5⅜ × 8½. 20094-9 Pa. $7.95

HISTORY OF PHILOSOPHY, Julián Marías. Clearest one-volume history on the market. Every major philosopher and dozens of others, to Existentialism and later. 505pp. 5⅜ × 8½. 21739-6 Pa. $9.95

ALL ABOUT LIGHTNING, Martin A. Uman. Highly readable non-technical survey of nature and causes of lightning, thunderstorms, ball lightning, St. Elmo's Fire, much more. Illustrated. 192pp. 5⅜ × 8½. 25237-X Pa. $5.95

SAILING ALONE AROUND THE WORLD, Captain Joshua Slocum. First man to sail around the world, alone, in small boat. One of great feats of seamanship told in delightful manner. 67 illustrations. 294pp. 5⅜ × 8½. 20326-3 Pa. $4.95

LETTERS AND NOTES ON THE MANNERS, CUSTOMS AND CONDITIONS OF THE NORTH AMERICAN INDIANS, George Catlin. Classic account of life among Plains Indians: ceremonies, hunt, warfare, etc. 312 plates. 572pp. of text. 6⅛ × 9¼. 22118-0, 22119-9, Pa. Two-vol. set $17.90

ALASKA: The Harriman Expedition, 1899, John Burroughs, John Muir, et al. Informative, engrossing accounts of two-month, 9,000-mile expedition. Native peoples, wildlife, forests, geography, salmon industry, glaciers, more. Profusely illustrated. 240 black-and-white line drawings. 124 black-and-white photographs. 3 maps. Index. 576pp. 5⅜ × 8½. 25109-8 Pa. $11.95

THE BOOK OF BEASTS: Being a Translation from a Latin Bestiary of the Twelfth Century, T. H. White. Wonderful catalog real and fanciful beasts: manticore, griffin, phoenix, amphivius, jaculus, many more. White's witty erudite commentary on scientific, historical aspects. Fascinating glimpse of medieval mind. Illustrated. 296pp. 5⅜ × 8¼. (Available in U.S. only) 24609-4 Pa. $6.95

FRANK LLOYD WRIGHT: ARCHITECTURE AND NATURE With 160 Illustrations, Donald Hoffmann. Profusely illustrated study of influence of nature—especially prairie—on Wright's designs for Fallingwater, Robie House, Guggenheim Museum, other masterpieces. 96pp. 9¼ × 10¾. 25098-9 Pa. $8.95

FRANK LLOYD WRIGHT'S FALLINGWATER, Donald Hoffmann. Wright's famous waterfall house: planning and construction of organic idea. History of site, owners, Wright's personal involvement. Photographs of various stages of building. Preface by Edgar Kaufmann, Jr. 100 illustrations. 112pp. 9¼ × 10.
23671-4 Pa. $8.95

YEARS WITH FRANK LLOYD WRIGHT: Apprentice to Genius, Edgar Tafel. Insightful memoir by a former apprentice presents a revealing portrait of Wright the man, the inspired teacher, the greatest American architect. 372 black-and-white illustrations. Preface. Index. vi + 228pp. 8¼ × 11. 24801-1 Pa. $10.95

THE STORY OF KING ARTHUR AND HIS KNIGHTS, Howard Pyle. Enchanting version of King Arthur fable has delighted generations with imaginative narratives of exciting adventures and unforgettable illustrations by the author. 41 illustrations. xviii + 313pp. 6⅛ × 9¼. 21445-1 Pa. $6.95

THE GODS OF THE EGYPTIANS, E. A. Wallis Budge. Thorough coverage of numerous gods of ancient Egypt by foremost Egyptologist. Information on evolution of cults, rites and gods; the cult of Osiris; the Book of the Dead and its rites; the sacred animals and birds; Heaven and Hell; and more. 956pp. 6⅛ × 9¼.
22055-9, 22056-7 Pa., Two-vol. set $21.90

A THEOLOGICO-POLITICAL TREATISE, Benedict Spinoza. Also contains unfinished *Political Treatise*. Great classic on religious liberty, theory of government on common consent. R. Elwes translation. Total of 421pp. 5⅜ × 8½.
20249-6 Pa. $7.95

INCIDENTS OF TRAVEL IN CENTRAL AMERICA, CHIAPAS, AND YUCATAN, John L. Stephens. Almost single-handed discovery of Maya culture; exploration of ruined cities, monuments, temples; customs of Indians. 115 drawings. 892pp. 5⅜ × 8½. 22404-X, 22405-8 Pa., Two-vol. set $15.90

LOS CAPRICHOS, Francisco Goya. 80 plates of wild, grotesque monsters and caricatures. Prado manuscript included. 183pp. 6⅝ × 9⅝. 22384-1 Pa. $5.95

AUTOBIOGRAPHY: The Story of My Experiments with Truth, Mohandas K. Gandhi. Not hagiography, but Gandhi in his own words. Boyhood, legal studies, purification, the growth of the Satyagraha (nonviolent protest) movement. Critical, inspiring work of the man who freed India. 480pp. 5⅜ × 8½. (Available in U.S. only)
24593-4 Pa. $6.95

ILLUSTRATED DICTIONARY OF HISTORIC ARCHITECTURE, edited by Cyril M. Harris. Extraordinary compendium of clear, concise definitions for over 5,000 important architectural terms complemented by over 2,000 line drawings. Covers full spectrum of architecture from ancient ruins to 20th-century Modernism. Preface. 592pp. 7½ × 9⅝. 24444-X Pa. $15.95

THE NIGHT BEFORE CHRISTMAS, Clement Moore. Full text, and woodcuts from original 1848 book. Also critical, historical material. 19 illustrations. 40pp. 4⅝ × 6. 22797-9 Pa. $2.50

THE LESSON OF JAPANESE ARCHITECTURE: 165 Photographs, Jiro Harada. Memorable gallery of 165 photographs taken in the 1930's of exquisite Japanese homes of the well-to-do and historic buildings. 13 line diagrams. 192pp. 8⅜ × 11¼. 24778-3 Pa. $10.95

THE AUTOBIOGRAPHY OF CHARLES DARWIN AND SELECTED LETTERS, edited by Francis Darwin. The fascinating life of eccentric genius composed of an intimate memoir by Darwin (intended for his children); commentary by his son, Francis; hundreds of fragments from notebooks, journals, papers; and letters to and from Lyell, Hooker, Huxley, Wallace and Henslow. xi + 365pp. 5⅜ × 8. 20479-0 Pa. $6.95

WONDERS OF THE SKY: Observing Rainbows, Comets, Eclipses, the Stars and Other Phenomena, Fred Schaaf. Charming, easy-to-read poetic guide to all manner of celestial events visible to the naked eye. Mock suns, glories, Belt of Venus, more. Illustrated. 299pp. 5¼ × 8¼. 24402-4 Pa. $7.95

BURNHAM'S CELESTIAL HANDBOOK, Robert Burnham, Jr. Thorough guide to the stars beyond our solar system. Exhaustive treatment. Alphabetical by constellation: Andromeda to Cetus in Vol. 1; Chamaeleon to Orion in Vol. 2; and Pavo to Vulpecula in Vol. 3. Hundreds of illustrations. Index in Vol. 3. 2,000pp. 6⅛ × 9¼. 23567-X, 23568-8, 23673-0 Pa., Three-vol. set $41.85

STAR NAMES: Their Lore and Meaning, Richard Hinckley Allen. Fascinating history of names various cultures have given to constellations and literary and folkloristic uses that have been made of stars. Indexes to subjects. Arabic and Greek names. Biblical references. Bibliography. 563pp. 5⅜ × 8½. 21079-0 Pa. $8.95

THIRTY YEARS THAT SHOOK PHYSICS: The Story of Quantum Theory, George Gamow. Lucid, accessible introduction to influential theory of energy and matter. Careful explanations of Dirac's anti-particles, Bohr's model of the atom, much more. 12 plates. Numerous drawings. 240pp. 5⅜ × 8½. 24895-X Pa. $5.95

CHINESE DOMESTIC FURNITURE IN PHOTOGRAPHS AND MEASURED DRAWINGS, Gustav Ecke. A rare volume, now affordably priced for antique collectors, furniture buffs and art historians. Detailed review of styles ranging from early Shang to late Ming. Unabridged republication. 161 black-and-white drawings, photos. Total of 224pp. 8⅜ × 11¼. (Available in U.S. only) 25171-3 Pa. $13.95

VINCENT VAN GOGH: A Biography, Julius Meier-Graefe. Dynamic, penetrating study of artist's life, relationship with brother, Theo, painting techniques, travels, more. Readable, engrossing. 160pp. 5⅜ × 8½. (Available in U.S. only) 25253-1 Pa. $4.95

HOW TO WRITE, Gertrude Stein. Gertrude Stein claimed anyone could understand her unconventional writing—here are clues to help. Fascinating improvisations, language experiments, explanations illuminate Stein's craft and the art of writing. Total of 414pp. 4⅜ × 6⅜. 23144-5 Pa. $6.95

ADVENTURES AT SEA IN THE GREAT AGE OF SAIL: Five Firsthand Narratives, edited by Elliot Snow. Rare true accounts of exploration, whaling, shipwreck, fierce natives, trade, shipboard life, more. 33 illustrations. Introduction. 353pp. 5⅜ × 8½. 25177-2 Pa. $8.95

THE HERBAL OR GENERAL HISTORY OF PLANTS, John Gerard. Classic descriptions of about 2,850 plants—with over 2,700 illustrations—includes Latin and English names, physical descriptions, varieties, time and place of growth, more. 2,706 illustrations. xlv + 1,678pp. 8½ × 12¼. 23147-X Cloth. $75.00

DOROTHY AND THE WIZARD IN OZ, L. Frank Baum. Dorothy and the Wizard visit the center of the Earth, where people are vegetables, glass houses grow and Oz characters reappear. Classic sequel to *Wizard of Oz*. 256pp. 5⅜ × 8. 24714-7 Pa. $5.95

SONGS OF EXPERIENCE: Facsimile Reproduction with 26 Plates in Full Color, William Blake. This facsimile of Blake's original "Illuminated Book" reproduces 26 full-color plates from a rare 1826 edition. Includes "The Tyger," "London," "Holy Thursday," and other immortal poems. 26 color plates. Printed text of poems. 48pp. 5¼ × 7. 24636-1 Pa. $3.95

SONGS OF INNOCENCE, William Blake. The first and most popular of Blake's famous "Illuminated Books," in a facsimile edition reproducing all 31 brightly colored plates. Additional printed text of each poem. 64pp. 5¼ × 7. 22764-2 Pa. $3.95

PRECIOUS STONES, Max Bauer. Classic, thorough study of diamonds, rubies, emeralds, garnets, etc.: physical character, occurrence, properties, use, similar topics. 20 plates, 8 in color. 94 figures. 659pp. 6⅛ × 9¼. 21910-0, 21911-9 Pa., Two-vol. set $15.90

ENCYCLOPEDIA OF VICTORIAN NEEDLEWORK, S. F. A. Caulfeild and Blanche Saward. Full, precise descriptions of stitches, techniques for dozens of needlecrafts—most exhaustive reference of its kind. Over 800 figures. Total of 679pp. 8⅛ × 11. Two volumes. Vol. 1 22800-2 Pa. $11.95
Vol. 2 22801-0 Pa. $11.95

THE MARVELOUS LAND OF OZ, L. Frank Baum. Second Oz book, the Scarecrow and Tin Woodman are back with hero named Tip, Oz magic. 136 illustrations. 287pp. 5⅜ × 8½. 20692-0 Pa. $5.95

WILD FOWL DECOYS, Joel Barber. Basic book on the subject, by foremost authority and collector. Reveals history of decoy making and rigging, place in American culture, different kinds of decoys, how to make them, and how to use them. 140 plates. 156pp. 7⅞ × 10¾. 20011-6 Pa. $8.95

HISTORY OF LACE, Mrs. Bury Palliser. Definitive, profusely illustrated chronicle of lace from earliest times to late 19th century. Laces of Italy, Greece, England, France, Belgium, etc. Landmark of needlework scholarship. 266 illustrations. 672pp. 6⅛ × 9¼. 24742-2 Pa. $14.95

ILLUSTRATED GUIDE TO SHAKER FURNITURE, Robert Meader. All furniture and appurtenances, with much on unknown local styles. 235 photos. 146pp. 9 × 12. 22819-3 Pa. $8.95

WHALE SHIPS AND WHALING: A Pictorial Survey, George Francis Dow. Over 200 vintage engravings, drawings, photographs of barks, brigs, cutters, other vessels. Also harpoons, lances, whaling guns, many other artifacts. Comprehensive text by foremost authority. 207 black-and-white illustrations. 288pp. 6 × 9. 24808-9 Pa. $9.95

THE BERTRAMS, Anthony Trollope. Powerful portrayal of blind self-will and thwarted ambition includes one of Trollope's most heartrending love stories. 497pp. 5⅜ × 8½. 25119-5 Pa. $9.95

ADVENTURES WITH A HAND LENS, Richard Headstrom. Clearly written guide to observing and studying flowers and grasses, fish scales, moth and insect wings, egg cases, buds, feathers, seeds, leaf scars, moss, molds, ferns, common crystals, etc.—all with an ordinary, inexpensive magnifying glass. 209 exact line drawings aid in your discoveries. 220pp. 5⅜ × 8½. 23330-8 Pa. $4.95

RODIN ON ART AND ARTISTS, Auguste Rodin. Great sculptor's candid, wide-ranging comments on meaning of art; great artists; relation of sculpture to poetry, painting, music; philosophy of life, more. 76 superb black-and-white illustrations of Rodin's sculpture, drawings and prints. 119pp. 8⅝ × 11¼. 24487-3 Pa. $7.95

FIFTY CLASSIC FRENCH FILMS, 1912–1982: A Pictorial Record, Anthony Slide. Memorable stills from Grand Illusion, Beauty and the Beast, Hiroshima, Mon Amour, many more. Credits, plot synopses, reviews, etc. 160pp. 8¼ × 11. 25256-6 Pa. $11.95

THE PRINCIPLES OF PSYCHOLOGY, William James. Famous long course complete, unabridged. Stream of thought, time perception, memory, experimental methods; great work decades ahead of its time. 94 figures. 1,391pp. 5⅜ × 8½. 20381-6, 20382-4 Pa., Two-vol. set $23.90

BODIES IN A BOOKSHOP, R. T. Campbell. Challenging mystery of blackmail and murder with ingenious plot and superbly drawn characters. In the best tradition of British suspense fiction. 192pp. 5⅜ × 8½. 24720-1 Pa. $4.95

CALLAS: PORTRAIT OF A PRIMA DONNA, George Jellinek. Renowned commentator on the musical scene chronicles incredible career and life of the most controversial, fascinating, influential operatic personality of our time. 64 black-and-white photographs. 416pp. 5⅜ × 8¼. 25047-4 Pa. $8.95

GEOMETRY, RELATIVITY AND THE FOURTH DIMENSION, Rudolph Rucker. Exposition of fourth dimension, concepts of relativity as Flatland characters continue adventures. Popular, easily followed yet accurate, profound. 141 illustrations. 133pp. 5⅜ × 8½. 23400-2 Pa. $4.95

HOUSEHOLD STORIES BY THE BROTHERS GRIMM, with pictures by Walter Crane. 53 classic stories—Rumpelstiltskin, Rapunzel, Hansel and Gretel, the Fisherman and his Wife, Snow White, Tom Thumb, Sleeping Beauty, Cinderella, and so much more—lavishly illustrated with original 19th century drawings. 114 illustrations. x + 269pp. 5⅜ × 8½. 21080-4 Pa. $4.95

SUNDIALS, Albert Waugh. Far and away the best, most thorough coverage of ideas, mathematics concerned, types, construction, adjusting anywhere. Over 100 illustrations. 230pp. 5⅜ × 8½. 22947-5 Pa. $5.95

PICTURE HISTORY OF THE NORMANDIE: With 190 Illustrations, Frank O. Braynard. Full story of legendary French ocean liner: Art Deco interiors, design innovations, furnishings, celebrities, maiden voyage, tragic fire, much more. Extensive text. 144pp. 8⅞ × 11¾. 25257-4 Pa. $10.95

THE FIRST AMERICAN COOKBOOK: A Facsimile of "American Cookery," 1796, Amelia Simmons. Facsimile of the first American-written cookbook published in the United States contains authentic recipes for colonial favorites—pumpkin pudding, winter squash pudding, spruce beer, Indian slapjacks, and more. Introductory Essay and Glossary of colonial cooking terms. 80pp. 5⅜ × 8½. 24710-4 Pa. $3.50

101 PUZZLES IN THOUGHT AND LOGIC, C. R. Wylie, Jr. Solve murders and robberies, find out which fishermen are liars, how a blind man could possibly identify a color—purely by your own reasoning! 107pp. 5⅜ × 8½. 20367-0 Pa. $2.50

ANCIENT EGYPTIAN MYTHS AND LEGENDS, Lewis Spence. Examines animism, totemism, fetishism, creation myths, deities, alchemy, art and magic, other topics. Over 50 illustrations. 432pp. 5⅜ × 8½. 26525-0 Pa. $8.95

ANTHROPOLOGY AND MODERN LIFE, Franz Boas. Great anthropologist's classic treatise on race and culture. Introduction by Ruth Bunzel. Only inexpensive paperback edition. 255pp. 5⅜ × 8½. 25245-0 Pa. $6.95

THE TALE OF PETER RABBIT, Beatrix Potter. The inimitable Peter's terrifying adventure in Mr. McGregor's garden, with all 27 wonderful, full-color Potter illustrations. 55pp. 4¼ × 5½. (Available in U.S. only) 22827-4 Pa. $1.75

THREE PROPHETIC SCIENCE FICTION NOVELS, H. G. Wells. *When the Sleeper Wakes, A Story of the Days to Come* and *The Time Machine* (full version). 335pp. 5⅜ × 8½. (Available in U.S. only) 20605-X Pa. $6.95

APICIUS COOKERY AND DINING IN IMPERIAL ROME, edited and translated by Joseph Dommers Vehling. Oldest known cookbook in existence offers readers a clear picture of what foods Romans ate, how they prepared them, etc. 49 illustrations. 301pp. 6⅛ × 9¼. 23563-7 Pa. $7.95

SHAKESPEARE LEXICON AND QUOTATION DICTIONARY, Alexander Schmidt. Full definitions, locations, shades of meaning of every word in plays and poems. More than 50,000 exact quotations. 1,485pp. 6½ × 9¼. 22726-X, 22727-8 Pa., Two-vol. set $31.90

THE WORLD'S GREAT SPEECHES, edited by Lewis Copeland and Lawrence W. Lamm. Vast collection of 278 speeches from Greeks to 1970. Powerful and effective models; unique look at history. 842pp. 5⅜ × 8½. 20468-5 Pa. $12.95

THE BLUE FAIRY BOOK, Andrew Lang. The first, most famous collection, with many familiar tales: Little Red Riding Hood, Aladdin and the Wonderful Lamp, Puss in Boots, Sleeping Beauty, Hansel and Gretel, Rumpelstiltskin; 37 in all. 138 illustrations. 390pp. 5⅜ × 8½. 21437-0 Pa. $6.95

THE STORY OF THE CHAMPIONS OF THE ROUND TABLE, Howard Pyle. Sir Launcelot, Sir Tristram and Sir Percival in spirited adventures of love and triumph retold in Pyle's inimitable style. 50 drawings, 31 full-page. xviii + 329pp. 6½ × 9¼. 21883-X Pa. $7.95

THE MYTHS OF THE NORTH AMERICAN INDIANS, Lewis Spence. Myths and legends of the Algonquins, Iroquois, Pawnees and Sioux with comprehensive historical and ethnological commentary. 36 illustrations. 5⅜ × 8½.
25967-6 Pa. $8.95

GREAT DINOSAUR HUNTERS AND THEIR DISCOVERIES, Edwin H. Colbert. Fascinating, lavishly illustrated chronicle of dinosaur research, 1820's to 1960. Achievements of Cope, Marsh, Brown, Buckland, Mantell, Huxley, many others. 384pp. 5¼ × 8¼. 24701-5 Pa. $7.95

THE TASTEMAKERS, Russell Lynes. Informal, illustrated social history of American taste 1850's–1950's. First popularized categories Highbrow, Lowbrow, Middlebrow. 129 illustrations. New (1979) afterword. 384pp. 6 × 9.
23993-4 Pa. $8.95

DOUBLE CROSS PURPOSES, Ronald A. Knox. A treasure hunt in the Scottish Highlands, an old map, unidentified corpse, surprise discoveries keep reader guessing in this cleverly intricate tale of financial skullduggery. 2 black-and-white maps. 320pp. 5⅜ × 8½. (Available in U.S. only) 25032-6 Pa. $6.95

AUTHENTIC VICTORIAN DECORATION AND ORNAMENTATION IN FULL COLOR: 46 Plates from "Studies in Design," Christopher Dresser. Superb full-color lithographs reproduced from rare original portfolio of a major Victorian designer. 48pp. 9¼ × 12¼. 25083-0 Pa. $7.95

PRIMITIVE ART, Franz Boas. Remains the best text ever prepared on subject, thoroughly discussing Indian, African, Asian, Australian, and, especially, Northern American primitive art. Over 950 illustrations show ceramics, masks, totem poles, weapons, textiles, paintings, much more. 376pp. 5⅜ × 8. 20025-6 Pa. $7.95

SIDELIGHTS ON RELATIVITY, Albert Einstein. Unabridged republication of two lectures delivered by the great physicist in 1920–21. *Ether and Relativity* and *Geometry and Experience*. Elegant ideas in non-mathematical form, accessible to intelligent layman. vi + 56pp. 5⅜ × 8½. 24511-X Pa. $2.95

THE WIT AND HUMOR OF OSCAR WILDE, edited by Alvin Redman. More than 1,000 ripostes, paradoxes, wisecracks: Work is the curse of the drinking classes, I can resist everything except temptation, etc. 258pp. 5⅜ × 8½. 20602-5 Pa. $4.95

ADVENTURES WITH A MICROSCOPE, Richard Headstrom. 59 adventures with clothing fibers, protozoa, ferns and lichens, roots and leaves, much more. 142 illustrations. 232pp. 5⅜ × 8½. 23471-1 Pa. $3.95

PLANTS OF THE BIBLE, Harold N. Moldenke and Alma L. Moldenke. Standard reference to all 230 plants mentioned in Scriptures. Latin name, biblical reference, uses, modern identity, much more. Unsurpassed encyclopedic resource for scholars, botanists, nature lovers, students of Bible. Bibliography. Indexes. 123 black-and-white illustrations. 384pp. 6 × 9. 25069-5 Pa. $8.95

FAMOUS AMERICAN WOMEN: A Biographical Dictionary from Colonial Times to the Present, Robert McHenry, ed. From Pocahontas to Rosa Parks, 1,035 distinguished American women documented in separate biographical entries. Accurate, up-to-date data, numerous categories, spans 400 years. Indices. 493pp. 6½ × 9¼. 24523-3 Pa. $10.95

THE FABULOUS INTERIORS OF THE GREAT OCEAN LINERS IN HISTORIC PHOTOGRAPHS, William H. Miller, Jr. Some 200 superb photographs capture exquisite interiors of world's great "floating palaces"—1890's to 1980's: *Titanic, Ile de France, Queen Elizabeth, United States, Europa,* more. Approx. 200 black-and-white photographs. Captions. Text. Introduction. 160pp. 8⅜ × 11¼. 24756-2 Pa. $9.95

THE GREAT LUXURY LINERS, 1927–1954: A Photographic Record, William H. Miller, Jr. Nostalgic tribute to heyday of ocean liners. 186 photos of Ile de France, Normandie, Leviathan, Queen Elizabeth, United States, many others. Interior and exterior views. Introduction. Captions. 160pp. 9 × 12. 24056-8 Pa. $10.95

A NATURAL HISTORY OF THE DUCKS, John Charles Phillips. Great landmark of ornithology offers complete detailed coverage of nearly 200 species and subspecies of ducks: gadwall, sheldrake, merganser, pintail, many more. 74 full-color plates, 102 black-and-white. Bibliography. Total of 1,920pp. 8⅜ × 11¼. 25141-1, 25142-X Cloth. Two-vol. set $100.00

THE SEAWEED HANDBOOK: An Illustrated Guide to Seaweeds from North Carolina to Canada, Thomas F. Lee. Concise reference covers 78 species. Scientific and common names, habitat, distribution, more. Finding keys for easy identification. 224pp. 5⅜ × 8½. 25215-9 Pa. $6.95

THE TEN BOOKS OF ARCHITECTURE: The 1755 Leoni Edition, Leon Battista Alberti. Rare classic helped introduce the glories of ancient architecture to the Renaissance. 68 black-and-white plates. 336pp. 8⅜ × 11¼. 25239-6 Pa. $14.95

MISS MACKENZIE, Anthony Trollope. Minor masterpieces by Victorian master unmasks many truths about life in 19th-century England. First inexpensive edition in years. 392pp. 5⅜ × 8½. 25201-9 Pa. $8.95

THE RIME OF THE ANCIENT MARINER, Gustave Doré, Samuel Taylor Coleridge. Dramatic engravings considered by many to be his greatest work. The terrifying space of the open sea, the storms and whirlpools of an unknown ocean, the ice of Antarctica, more—all rendered in a powerful, chilling manner. Full text. 38 plates. 77pp. 9¼ × 12. 22305-1 Pa. $4.95

THE EXPEDITIONS OF ZEBULON MONTGOMERY PIKE, Zebulon Montgomery Pike. Fascinating first-hand accounts (1805–6) of exploration of Mississippi River, Indian wars, capture by Spanish dragoons, much more. 1,088pp. 5⅜ × 8½. 25254-X, 25255-8 Pa. Two-vol. set $25.90

A CONCISE HISTORY OF PHOTOGRAPHY: Third Revised Edition, Helmut Gernsheim. Best one-volume history—camera obscura, photochemistry, daguerreotypes, evolution of cameras, film, more. Also artistic aspects—landscape, portraits, fine art, etc. 281 black-and-white photographs. 26 in color. 176pp. 8⅜ × 11¼. 25128-4 Pa. $13.95

THE DORÉ BIBLE ILLUSTRATIONS, Gustave Doré. 241 detailed plates from the Bible: the Creation scenes, Adam and Eve, Flood, Babylon, battle sequences, life of Jesus, etc. Each plate is accompanied by the verses from the King James version of the Bible. 241pp. 9 × 12. 23004-X Pa. $9.95

WANDERINGS IN WEST AFRICA, Richard F. Burton. Great Victorian scholar/adventurer's invaluable descriptions of African tribal rituals, fetishism, culture, art, much more. Fascinating 19th-century account. 624pp. 5⅜ × 8½. 26890-X Pa. $12.95

FLATLAND, E. A. Abbott. Intriguing and enormously popular science-fiction classic explores the complexities of trying to survive as a two-dimensional being in a three-dimensional world. Amusingly illustrated by the author. 16 illustrations. 103pp. 5⅜ × 8½. 20001-9 Pa. $2.50

THE HISTORY OF THE LEWIS AND CLARK EXPEDITION, Meriwether Lewis and William Clark, edited by Elliott Coues. Classic edition of Lewis and Clark's day-by-day journals that later became the basis for U.S. claims to Oregon and the West. Accurate and invaluable geographical, botanical, biological, meteorological and anthropological material. Total of 1,508pp. 5⅜ × 8½.
21268-8, 21269-6, 21270-X Pa. Three-vol. set $26.85

LANGUAGE, TRUTH AND LOGIC, Alfred J. Ayer. Famous, clear introduction to Vienna, Cambridge schools of Logical Positivism. Role of philosophy, elimination of metaphysics, nature of analysis, etc. 160pp. 5⅜ × 8½. (Available in U.S. and Canada only) 20010-8 Pa. $3.95

MATHEMATICS FOR THE NONMATHEMATICIAN, Morris Kline. Detailed, college-level treatment of mathematics in cultural and historical context, with numerous exercises. For liberal arts students. Preface. Recommended Reading Lists. Tables. Index. Numerous black-and-white figures. xvi + 641pp. 5⅜ × 8½.
24823-2 Pa. $11.95

HANDBOOK OF PICTORIAL SYMBOLS, Rudolph Modley. 3,250 signs and symbols, many systems in full; official or heavy commercial use. Arranged by subject. Most in Pictorial Archive series. 143pp. 8⅛ × 11. 23357-X Pa. $6.95

INCIDENTS OF TRAVEL IN YUCATAN, John L. Stephens. Classic (1843) exploration of jungles of Yucatan, looking for evidences of Maya civilization. Travel adventures, Mexican and Indian culture, etc. Total of 669pp. 5⅜ × 8½.
20926-1, 20927-X Pa., Two-vol. set $11.90

DEGAS: An Intimate Portrait, Ambroise Vollard. Charming, anecdotal memoir by famous art dealer of one of the greatest 19th-century French painters. 14 black-and-white illustrations. Introduction by Harold L. Van Doren. 96pp. 5⅜ × 8½.
25131-4 Pa. $4.95

PERSONAL NARRATIVE OF A PILGRIMAGE TO ALMANDINAH AND MECCAH, Richard Burton. Great travel classic by remarkably colorful personality. Burton, disguised as a Moroccan, visited sacred shrines of Islam, narrowly escaping death. 47 illustrations. 959pp. 5⅜ × 8½.   21217-3, 21218-1 Pa., Two-vol. set $19.90

PHRASE AND WORD ORIGINS, A. H. Holt. Entertaining, reliable, modern study of more than 1,200 colorful words, phrases, origins and histories. Much unexpected information. 254pp. 5⅜ × 8½.   20758-7 Pa. $5.95

THE RED THUMB MARK, R. Austin Freeman. In this first Dr. Thorndyke case, the great scientific detective draws fascinating conclusions from the nature of a single fingerprint. Exciting story, authentic science. 320pp. 5⅜ × 8½. (Available in U.S. only)   25210-8 Pa. $6.95

AN EGYPTIAN HIEROGLYPHIC DICTIONARY, E. A. Wallis Budge. Monumental work containing about 25,000 words or terms that occur in texts ranging from 3000 B.C. to 600 A.D. Each entry consists of a transliteration of the word, the word in hieroglyphs, and the meaning in English. 1,314pp. 6⅜ × 10.
23615-3, 23616-1 Pa., Two-vol. set $35.90

THE COMPLEAT STRATEGYST: Being a Primer on the Theory of Games of Strategy, J. D. Williams. Highly entertaining classic describes, with many illustrated examples, how to select best strategies in conflict situations. Prefaces. Appendices. xvi + 268pp. 5⅜ × 8½.   25101-2 Pa. $6.95

THE ROAD TO OZ, L. Frank Baum. Dorothy meets the Shaggy Man, little Button-Bright and the Rainbow's beautiful daughter in this delightful trip to the magical Land of Oz. 272pp. 5⅜ × 8.   25208-6 Pa. $5.95

POINT AND LINE TO PLANE, Wassily Kandinsky. Seminal exposition of role of point, line, other elements in non-objective painting. Essential to understanding 20th-century art. 127 illustrations. 192pp. 6½ × 9¼.   23808-3 Pa. $5.95

LADY ANNA, Anthony Trollope. Moving chronicle of Countess Lovel's bitter struggle to win for herself and daughter Anna their rightful rank and fortune— perhaps at cost of sanity itself. 384pp. 5⅜ × 8½.   24669-8 Pa. $8.95

EGYPTIAN MAGIC, E. A. Wallis Budge. Sums up all that is known about magic in Ancient Egypt: the role of magic in controlling the gods, powerful amulets that warded off evil spirits, scarabs of immortality, use of wax images, formulas and spells, the secret name, much more. 253pp. 5⅜ × 8½.   22681-6 Pa. $4.50

THE DANCE OF SIVA, Ananda Coomaraswamy. Preeminent authority unfolds the vast metaphysic of India: the revelation of her art, conception of the universe, social organization, etc. 27 reproductions of art masterpieces. 192pp. 5⅜ × 8½.
24817-8 Pa. $5.95

CHRISTMAS CUSTOMS AND TRADITIONS, Clement A. Miles. Origin, evolution, significance of religious, secular practices. Caroling, gifts, yule logs, much more. Full, scholarly yet fascinating; non-sectarian. 400pp. 5⅜ × 8½.

23354-5 Pa. $6.95

THE HUMAN FIGURE IN MOTION, Eadweard Muybridge. More than 4,500 stopped-action photos, in action series, showing undraped men, women, children jumping, lying down, throwing, sitting, wrestling, carrying, etc. 390pp. 7⅞ × 10⅝.

20204-6 Cloth. $24.95

THE MAN WHO WAS THURSDAY, Gilbert Keith Chesterton. Witty, fast-paced novel about a club of anarchists in turn-of-the-century London. Brilliant social, religious, philosophical speculations. 128pp. 5⅜ × 8½.   25121-7 Pa. $3.95

A CEZANNE SKETCHBOOK: Figures, Portraits, Landscapes and Still Lifes, Paul Cezanne. Great artist experiments with tonal effects, light, mass, other qualities in over 100 drawings. A revealing view of developing master painter, precursor of Cubism. 102 black-and-white illustrations. 144pp. 8¾ × 6⅝.   24790-2 Pa. $6.95

AN ENCYCLOPEDIA OF BATTLES: Accounts of Over 1,560 Battles from 1479 B.C. to the Present, David Eggenberger. Presents essential details of every major battle in recorded history, from the first battle of Megiddo in 1479 B.C. to Grenada in 1984. List of Battle Maps. New Appendix covering the years 1967–1984. Index. 99 illustrations. 544pp. 6½ × 9¼.   24913-1 Pa. $14.95

AN ETYMOLOGICAL DICTIONARY OF MODERN ENGLISH, Ernest Weekley. Richest, fullest work, by foremost British lexicographer. Detailed word histories. Inexhaustible. Total of 856pp. 6½ × 9¼.

21873-2, 21874-0 Pa., Two-vol. set $19.90

WEBSTER'S AMERICAN MILITARY BIOGRAPHIES, edited by Robert McHenry. Over 1,000 figures who shaped 3 centuries of American military history. Detailed biographies of Nathan Hale, Douglas MacArthur, Mary Hallaren, others. Chronologies of engagements, more. Introduction. Addenda. 1,033 entries in alphabetical order. xi + 548pp. 6½ × 9¼. (Available in U.S. only)

24758-9 Pa. $13.95

LIFE IN ANCIENT EGYPT, Adolf Erman. Detailed older account, with much not in more recent books: domestic life, religion, magic, medicine, commerce, and whatever else needed for complete picture. Many illustrations. 597pp. 5⅜ × 8½.

22632-8 Pa. $8.95

HISTORIC COSTUME IN PICTURES, Braun & Schneider. Over 1,450 costumed figures shown, covering a wide variety of peoples: kings, emperors, nobles, priests, servants, soldiers, scholars, townsfolk, peasants, merchants, courtiers, cavaliers, and more. 256pp. 8⅜ × 11¼.   23150-X Pa. $9.95

THE NOTEBOOKS OF LEONARDO DA VINCI, edited by J. P. Richter. Extracts from manuscripts reveal great genius; on painting, sculpture, anatomy, sciences, geography, etc. Both Italian and English. 186 ms. pages reproduced, plus 500 additional drawings, including studies for Last Supper, Sforza monument, etc. 860pp. 7⅞ × 10¾. (Available in U.S. only) 22572-0, 22573-9 Pa., Two-vol. set $31.90

THE ART NOUVEAU STYLE BOOK OF ALPHONSE MUCHA: All 72 Plates from "Documents Decoratifs" in Original Color, Alphonse Mucha. Rare copyright-free design portfolio by high priest of Art Nouveau. Jewelry, wallpaper, stained glass, furniture, figure studies, plant and animal motifs, etc. Only complete one-volume edition. 80pp. 9⅜ × 12¼. 24044-4 Pa. $9.95

ANIMALS: 1,419 COPYRIGHT-FREE ILLUSTRATIONS OF MAMMALS, BIRDS, FISH, INSECTS, ETC., edited by Jim Harter. Clear wood engravings present, in extremely lifelike poses, over 1,000 species of animals. One of the most extensive pictorial sourcebooks of its kind. Captions. Index. 284pp. 9 × 12. 23766-4 Pa. $9.95

OBELISTS FLY HIGH, C. Daly King. Masterpiece of American detective fiction, long out of print, involves murder on a 1935 transcontinental flight—"a very thrilling story"—NY Times. Unabridged and unaltered republication of the edition published by William Collins Sons & Co. Ltd., London, 1935. 288pp. 5⅜ × 8½. (Available in U.S. only) 25036-9 Pa. $5.95

VICTORIAN AND EDWARDIAN FASHION: A Photographic Survey, Alison Gernsheim. First fashion history completely illustrated by contemporary photographs. Full text plus 235 photos, 1840–1914, in which many celebrities appear. 240pp. 6½ × 9¼. 24205-6 Pa. $8.95

THE ART OF THE FRENCH ILLUSTRATED BOOK, 1700–1914, Gordon N. Ray. Over 630 superb book illustrations by Fragonard, Delacroix, Daumier, Doré, Grandville, Manet, Mucha, Steinlen, Toulouse-Lautrec and many others. Preface. Introduction. 633 halftones. Indices of artists, authors & titles, binders and provenances. Appendices. Bibliography. 608pp. 8⅜ × 11¼. 25086-5 Pa. $24.95

THE WONDERFUL WIZARD OF OZ, L. Frank Baum. Facsimile in full color of America's finest children's classic. 143 illustrations by W. W. Denslow. 267pp. 5⅜ × 8½. 20691-2 Pa. $7.95

FOLLOWING THE EQUATOR: A Journey Around the World, Mark Twain. Great writer's 1897 account of circumnavigating the globe by steamship. Ironic humor, keen observations, vivid and fascinating descriptions of exotic places. 197 illustrations. 720pp. 5⅜ × 8½. 26113-1 Pa. $15.95

THE FRIENDLY STARS, Martha Evans Martin & Donald Howard Menzel. Classic text marshalls the stars together in an engaging, non-technical survey, presenting them as sources of beauty in night sky. 23 illustrations. Foreword. 2 star charts. Index. 147pp. 5⅜ × 8½. 21099-5 Pa. $3.95

FADS AND FALLACIES IN THE NAME OF SCIENCE, Martin Gardner. Fair, witty appraisal of cranks, quacks, and quackeries of science and pseudoscience: hollow earth, Velikovsky, orgone energy, Dianetics, flying saucers, Bridey Murphy, food and medical fads, etc. Revised, expanded In the Name of Science. "A very able and even-tempered presentation."—The New Yorker. 363pp. 5⅜ × 8. 20394-8 Pa. $6.95

ANCIENT EGYPT: ITS CULTURE AND HISTORY, J. E Manchip White. From pre-dynastics through Ptolemies: society, history, political structure, religion, daily life, literature, cultural heritage. 48 plates. 217pp. 5⅜ × 8½. 22548-8 Pa. $5.95

CATALOG OF DOVER BOOKS

SIR HARRY HOTSPUR OF HUMBLETHWAITE, Anthony Trollope. Incisive, unconventional psychological study of a conflict between a wealthy baronet, his idealistic daughter, and their scapegrace cousin. The 1870 novel in its first inexpensive edition in years. 250pp. 5⅜ × 8½. 24953-0 Pa. $6.95

LASERS AND HOLOGRAPHY, Winston E. Kock. Sound introduction to burgeoning field, expanded (1981) for second edition. Wave patterns, coherence, lasers, diffraction, zone plates, properties of holograms, recent advances. 84 illustrations. 160pp. 5⅜ × 8¼. (Except in United Kingdom) 24041-X Pa. $3.95

INTRODUCTION TO ARTIFICIAL INTELLIGENCE: SECOND, ENLARGED EDITION, Philip C. Jackson, Jr. Comprehensive survey of artificial intelligence—the study of how machines (computers) can be made to act intelligently. Includes introductory and advanced material. Extensive notes updating the main text. 132 black-and-white illustrations. 512pp. 5⅜ × 8½. 24864-X Pa. $8.95

HISTORY OF INDIAN AND INDONESIAN ART, Ananda K. Coomaraswamy. Over 400 illustrations illuminate classic study of Indian art from earliest Harappa finds to early 20th century. Provides philosophical, religious and social insights. 304pp. 6⅝ × 9⅝. 25005-9 Pa. $11.95

THE GOLEM, Gustav Meyrink. Most famous supernatural novel in modern European literature, set in Ghetto of Old Prague around 1890. Compelling story of mystical experiences, strange transformations, profound terror. 13 black-and-white illustrations. 224pp. 5⅜ × 8½. (Available in U.S. only) 25025-3 Pa. $6.95

PICTORIAL ENCYCLOPEDIA OF HISTORIC ARCHITECTURAL PLANS, DETAILS AND ELEMENTS: With 1,880 Line Drawings of Arches, Domes, Doorways, Facades, Gables, Windows, etc., John Theodore Haneman. Sourcebook of inspiration for architects, designers, others. Bibliography. Captions. 141pp. 9 × 12. 24605-1 Pa. $7.95

BENCHLEY LOST AND FOUND, Robert Benchley. Finest humor from early 30's, about pet peeves, child psychologists, post office and others. Mostly unavailable elsewhere. 73 illustrations by Peter Arno and others. 183pp. 5⅜ × 8½. 22410-4 Pa. $4.95

ERTÉ GRAPHICS, Erté. Collection of striking color graphics: *Seasons, Alphabet, Numerals, Aces* and *Precious Stones*. 50 plates, including 4 on covers. 48pp. 9⅜ × 12¼. 23580-7 Pa. $7.95

THE JOURNAL OF HENRY D. THOREAU, edited by Bradford Torrey, F. H. Allen. Complete reprinting of 14 volumes, 1837–61, over two million words; the sourcebooks for *Walden*, etc. Definitive. All original sketches, plus 75 photographs. 1,804pp. 8½ × 12¼. 20312-3, 20313-1 Cloth., Two-vol. set $125.00

CASTLES: THEIR CONSTRUCTION AND HISTORY, Sidney Toy. Traces castle development from ancient roots. Nearly 200 photographs and drawings illustrate moats, keeps, baileys, many other features. Caernarvon, Dover Castles, Hadrian's Wall, Tower of London, dozens more. 256pp. 5⅜ × 8¼. 24898-4 Pa. $6.95

AMERICAN CLIPPER SHIPS: 1833–1858, Octavius T. Howe & Frederick C. Matthews. Fully-illustrated, encyclopedic review of 352 clipper ships from the period of America's greatest maritime supremacy. Introduction. 109 halftones. 5 black-and-white line illustrations. Index. Total of 928pp. 5⅜ × 8½.
25115-2, 25116-0 Pa., Two-vol. set $17.90

TOWARDS A NEW ARCHITECTURE, Le Corbusier. Pioneering manifesto by great architect, near legendary founder of "International School." Technical and aesthetic theories, views on industry, economics, relation of form to function, "mass-production spirit," much more. Profusely illustrated. Unabridged translation of 13th French edition. Introduction by Frederick Etchells. 320pp. 6⅛ × 9¼. (Available in U.S. only)
25023-7 Pa. $8.95

THE BOOK OF KELLS, edited by Blanche Cirker. Inexpensive collection of 32 full-color, full-page plates from the greatest illuminated manuscript of the Middle Ages, painstakingly reproduced from rare facsimile edition. Publisher's Note. Captions. 32pp. 9⅜ × 12¼.
24345-1 Pa. $4.95

BEST SCIENCE FICTION STORIES OF H. G. WELLS, H. G. Wells. Full novel The Invisible Man, plus 17 short stories: "The Crystal Egg," "Aepyornis Island," "The Strange Orchid," etc. 303pp. 5⅜ × 8½. (Available in U.S. only)
21531-8 Pa. $6.95

AMERICAN SAILING SHIPS: Their Plans and History, Charles G. Davis. Photos, construction details of schooners, frigates, clippers, other sailcraft of 18th to early 20th centuries—plus entertaining discourse on design, rigging, nautical lore, much more. 137 black-and-white illustrations. 240pp. 6⅛ × 9¼.
24658-2 Pa. $6.95

ENTERTAINING MATHEMATICAL PUZZLES, Martin Gardner. Selection of author's favorite conundrums involving arithmetic, money, speed, etc., with lively commentary. Complete solutions. 112pp. 5⅜ × 8½.
25211-6 Pa. $2.95

THE WILL TO BELIEVE, HUMAN IMMORTALITY, William James. Two books bound together. Effect of irrational on logical, and arguments for human immortality. 402pp. 5⅜ × 8½.
20291-7 Pa. $7.95

THE HAUNTED MONASTERY and THE CHINESE MAZE MURDERS, Robert Van Gulik. 2 full novels by Van Gulik continue adventures of Judge Dee and his companions. An evil Taoist monastery, seemingly supernatural events; overgrown topiary maze that hides strange crimes. Set in 7th-century China. 27 illustrations. 328pp. 5⅜ × 8½.
23502-5 Pa. $6.95

CELEBRATED CASES OF JUDGE DEE (DEE GOONG AN), translated by Robert Van Gulik. Authentic 18th-century Chinese detective novel; Dee and associates solve three interlocked cases. Led to Van Gulik's own stories with same characters. Extensive introduction. 9 illustrations. 237pp. 5⅜ × 8½.
23337-5 Pa. $5.95

Prices subject to change without notice.
Available at your book dealer or write for free catalog to Dept. GI, Dover Publications, Inc., 31 East 2nd St., Mineola, N.Y. 11501. Dover publishes more than 175 books each year on science, elementary and advanced mathematics, biology, music, art, literary history, social sciences and other areas.